MV✓✓

The Dictionary of the
Environment and Its Biomes

Chris Myers, Ph.D.
Miami University
General Editor

Marilee Foglesong

Former Young Adult Coordinator, New York Public Library

Paul L. Sieswerda

Curator, Aquarium for Wildlife Conservation

Advisers

DEVELOPED, DESIGNED, AND PRODUCED BY
BOOK BUILDERS LLC

Photographs © Archive Photos: 11, 121; 95 (Frank A. Cezus); 52 (Reuters/HO); 29 *right* (Reuters/Savita Kirloskar); 87 (Reuters/Sunil Malhotra); 114 (Reuters/Juan Carlos Ulate); 22 (Reuters/Arnd Weigmann); **Elyssa Kellerman:** 34, 80 *left* ; **Photo Researchers, Inc.:** 42 (Dr. Charles R. Belinky); 20 *right* (Bjorn Bolstad); 68 (John Chomack); 88 (Tim Davis); 106 (Gregory G. Dimijian); cover *top, far right* (Christine M. Douglas); 51 (William Ervin/Science Photos Library); 58 *right* (Douglas Faulkner); 80 *right* (Jack Fields); 115 (Simon Fraser/Northumbrian Environmental Mgmt. Ltd./Science Photo Library); 29 *left*, 102 (Georg Gerster); cover *top, near right* (Michael P. Gadomski); 44 (Francois Gohier); 104 (Ned Haines); 116 (H. Charles Laun); 64 (Pat and Tom Leeson); 83 (Tom McHugh); 55 (Will McIntyre); cover *top, far left* (Will and Deni McIntyre); 110 (YVA Momatiuk and John Eastcott); 33 (NASA/Science Source); 59 (Mark Newman); 73 (Porterfield/Chickering); 27 (G. Carleton Ray); 36, 62 (Earl Roberge); 82 (Blair Seitz); cover *bottom* (Jim Steinberg); 58 *left* (Stuart Westmorland); cover *top, near left* (Art Wolfe); **Anne Wertheim Rosenfeld:** 24; **Diane Shapiro:** 30, 50, 56, 70, 72, 77, 90, 92, 93, 108; **Wildlife Conservation Society:** 40. 46, 84, 120; 17, 48, 57, 66, 118 (M. Darocha); 9 *right*, 20 *left*, 39, 63 (D. DeMello); 6 (E. Kellerman); 7, 9 *left*, 37, 89 (B. Meng); 15 (C.A. Rogus); 61, 100, 122 (D. Shapiro); cover and interior design by **Ann Antoshak** for Book Builders.

Every endeavor has been made to obtain permission to use copyrighted material. The publishers would appreciate errors or omissions being brought to their attention.

Library of Congress Cataloging-in-Publication Data

The dictionary of the environment and its biomes.
    p. cm.
  "A Watts reference book."
  Includes bibliographical references (p.).
  ISBN 0-531-11983-1
    1. Biotic Communities—Dictionaries, Juvenile. [Biotic communities—Encyclopedia.] I. Franklin Watts, Inc.

QH540.4.D53 2001
577.8'2'03—dc21   00-065438

Contents

Note to the Reader

Think of the many ways we are connected to the environment. We depend on the environment for the food we eat, the clothes we wear, the fuel we use, and the medicines that cure us.

Within the environment of our planet there are different regions called biomes. These include the dry desert, the bone-chilling polar regions, the lush forests, and the deep, salty seas. Each of these biomes is home to marvelous creatures and plants that capture our imaginations.

Each type of biome is unique, but biomes are also linked to one another. Seaweed set adrift on ocean currents may land on islands and become food for marine iguanas. The air you breathe today may contain oxygen from the ancient giant trees of a tropical rain forest.

The Dictionary of the Environment and Its Biomes can help you discover fascinating facts and information about your immediate surroundings, as well as about some amazing far-away lands and animals. Although books such as this will raise some important questions, it is also important to go outside and explore on your own. If you have climbed a tree, collected berries, or walked in a stream, you have already taken the most important step toward learning more about the world in which you live.

How to Use This Book

The entries in *The Dictionary of the Environment and Its Biomes* are arranged in alphabetical order, from A to Z. They identify and explain a variety of topics related to the environment and environmental issues. You will find some entries that have only a title and a line that directs you to "see" another entry. You can turn to the other entry, where the topic you are researching is discussed.

Most entries in the dictionary contain *cross-references*. These are words or phrases in SMALL CAPITAL LETTERS that point to related subjects discussed elsewhere in the dictionary. Whenever you see a cross-reference, in either the text or at the end of an entry, you can find more information on that topic in a separate entry. The index at the back of the book will also help you locate related information.

Scattered throughout the dictionary are various special features, each of which is identified by a particular color and symbol. These features provide additional information for certain entries. One feature is "Biome Snapshot," which illustrates the most important elements and characteristics of each of Earth's *biomes*, or regions where climate, vegetation, and animal life are very similar. "Where Are They Found?" highlights certain species of plants or animals that live in a particular biome. The feature "Key Species" gives information on a plant or animal that is especially well adapted to its habitat, or surroundings. Finally, "Case Studies" shows how people or things have affected the environment.

At the end of the dictionary is a list of books and Web sites where you can find more information on environmental topics. There is also a list of major organizations and agencies that deal with environmental issues or do work related to the environment.

Note to the Educator

This dictionary provides an introduction to the world's biomes and covers key environmental concepts. The entries include concise definitions and overviews of important ecological regions, descriptions of various plants and animals, and information on pivotal environment issues, while also providing insights into the central biological, physical, and social forces that shape life on our Earth. Examples, extensive cross-references, and photographs help bring even difficult subjects to life.

Other lands fascinate young people. By emphasizing biomes in this dictionary, we hope to encourage a sense of place. Learning to appreciate the diversity of life, and how life is intimately tied to place, will help young readers discover some of the natural and inevitable lessons of the environment—the lessons of connection, including commonalities, integration, complexity, scale, and perspective.

Considering the environment makes one think of interdependence. Each of us shares our local environments with other people and other organisms. And all of us share one Earth. As citizens of this planet, one of our most vital undertakings will be to develop a deeper understanding of the place where we live. We hope that *The Dictionary of the Environment and Its Biomes* will bring readers a step closer to this goal.

Chris Myers

Acid Rain

A product of AIR POLLUTION characterized by an excess of sulfur and nitrogen gases in the ATMOSPHERE. These gases combine with moisture in the air to produce sulfuric and nitric acids, which are then deposited as rain and other forms of PRECIPITATION. The burning of fossil fuels, such as oil, contributes to acid rain by increasing the amount of sulfur in the atmosphere. When acid rain falls into lakes and ponds, the water can become so acidic that FISH and other ANIMALS cannot live in it.

Adaptation

An evolutionary change in a physical characteristic or a behavior of an ORGANISM that improves its chance of survival in a particular ENVIRONMENT. Organisms have different types of adaptations. The most obvious adaptations are structural; that is, they affect the physical structure of an organism. For example, the feet of ducks are webbed and allow these BIRDS to move quickly through water. A cardinal's feet have long, thin toes to help it perch on a tree branch.

Adaptations may also involve internal functions such as chemical processes. A PLANT's ability to make food through PHOTOSYNTHESIS is a physiological adaptation.

Case Study: Acid Rain in the Adirondacks

ACID RAIN is a serious problem in the Adirondack Mountains of New York, a region with nearly 3,000 lakes and ponds and millions of acres of FOREST. The Adirondack region is especially vulnerable to damage from acid rain. Its SOIL is thin and lacks minerals that can neutralize the acids in acid rain. The region has heavy snowfall, and spring runoff carries large amounts of acidic water into lakes and streams. The increased acidity in soil and water has harmed the region's FISH and TREES. Hundreds of Adirondack lakes can no longer support fish. On thousands of acres of Adirondack forest, trees also show signs of damage from acid rain.

The ability of chameleons to change color to match their surroundings is an adaptation that improves their chance of survival.

People usually think of ANIMALS in connection with behavioral adaptations, such as the seasonal migration of monarch butterflies between winter and summer HABITATS. But plants also exhibit behavioral adaptations, such as when they grow and bend toward sunlight.

In a particular BIOME, many different organisms may develop similar adaptations. An example of this is the large ears of ELEPHANTS, bat-eared foxes, and other animals in tropical regions. The large ears allow these animals to radiate heat away from their bodies.

Africa ❧ See CONTINENTS.

Agriculture ❧ The science or practice of growing PLANTS and raising ANIMALS to provide food, clothing, and other products that people need. Agriculture is often called *farming*.

Modern agriculture seeks to use technology to produce healthy crops and livestock without depleting the environment of valuable NATURAL RESOURCES, such as water and SOIL. Yet traditional farming methods may be more environmentally sound. For example, farmers in many areas of the world plant different crops each season in order not to deplete the soil of **nutrients**. [*See also* GENETIC ENGINEERING.]

Air Pollution ❧ Condition resulting from the addition of harmful substances to the ATMOSPHERE. Air pollution comes from different sources— factories, air conditioners, automobiles, and even natural processes such as FIRE and VOLCANOES. If allowed to go unchecked, air pollution can result in damage to the ENVIRONMENT and human health. For example, too much carbon dioxide in the atmosphere creates a GREENHOUSE EFFECT, which causes a warming effect in the environment. Some air pollution returns to the earth in the form of ACID RAIN and SMOG. Inhaling contaminated air can cause breathing problems and other health threats.

Algae

Simple, plantlike ORGANISMS found in water, SOIL, and on damp surfaces. Algae vary in size from a microscopic single cell to the 200-foot-giant kelp, a type of seaweed. Like PLANTS, algae produce their own food through PHOTOSYNTHESIS. Some types of algae live together in symbiosis with FUNGI to form LICHENS.

In MARINE BIOMES, algae form the base of the food web in the HABITATS of CORAL REEFS. Many marine animals, including a wide variety of FISH, feed on algae ranging in size from single-celled organisms called *diatoms* and tiny algae called *dinoflagellates* to the various varieties of seaweeds.

Altitude

The vertical distance of a feature, such as a MOUNTAIN or plateau, above mean sea level. It is also referred to as the *elevation*.

Environments vary according to the altitude. Different HABITATS occur as elevation changes. For example, at the base of a mountain in South America, the habitat may be a TROPICAL FOREST, home to many different SPECIES of BIRDS, REPTILES, and AMPHIBIANS. As the elevation increases up the mountainside, the habitats also change, and there will be fewer and often different species of ANIMALS and PLANTS. At the highest altitude on the sides and tops of the mountain, an area above the tree line, only small numbers of tiny plants grow and few animals can find food or shelter.

Amazon River

See FRESHWATER BIOMES.

Amphibians

A group of ANIMALS that have two distinct life stages: the larval and the adult. The word *amphibian* means "two lives."

Amphibians include salamanders, newts, FROGS, toads, and certain other SPECIES. Amphibians are found in almost every type of HABITAT except the POLAR REGIONS and very dry DESERTS.

All amphibians are COLD-BLOODED, which means that their

Frogs, such as this colorful species, are found in many habitats around the world.

Case Study: Water Music

Often we hear frogs before we see them. On an early spring night in northeastern United States, a woodland pond is filled with the calls of spring peepers—tiny green tree frogs. Springtime is breeding season in this TEMPERATE region, and like other frogs, spring peepers must lay their masses of eggs in water. So as soon as the ice begins to melt, these amphibians make their way to permanent and temporary pools. Most SPECIES of frogs locate mates by calling, and each species has its own special call. Later in the spring and summer, wood, green, and bullfrogs add their calls, creating a very loud chorus.

internal body temperature varies with their ENVIRONMENT. The skin of most amphibians helps the animals keep moisture in their bodies and aids in taking in oxygen. The skin must be kept moist by glands that secrete mucus.

Typically, amphibians begin life as eggs. Since the eggs do not have protective outer shells, amphibians lay their eggs in water or moist places. In most species of amphibians, the eggs hatch into larvae, early forms of amphibians that usually look different from the adult form. For example, the larvae of adult frogs are called *tadpoles*. Larvae develop into adults through a process called *metamor-*

phosis—a dramatic change in the form or structure of an animal.

Much of the WETLANDS habitat that amphibians live in has been lost due to human DEVELOPMENT. In addition, ACID RAIN, the GREENHOUSE EFFECT, and depletion of the OZONE layer may be contributing to declines in the numbers of amphibians around the globe. Because of their dependence on clean water and air, amphibians are sensitive to changes in their environment. The disappearance of amphibians is an indication that severe environmental problems exist.

Animals
⚘ Living ORGANISMS that usually have external or internal skeletons and muscles that allow them to move in search of food. Animals eat other organisms, while most PLANTS make their own food through a process called PHOTOSYNTHESIS.

There are about one and a half million known SPECIES of animals on earth, and scientists estimate that there may be as many as 30 million more that have not yet been identified. They inhabit all the earth's BIOMES, from the TUNDRA to MOUNTAINS to the OCEANS. Animals range in size from tiny, microscopic organisms to the world's largest MAMMAL, the 100-foot-long blue whale.

Animals are divided into two basic categories: VERTEBRATES, which include all organisms with a backbone, and INVERTEBRATES, which include all of the other animals. Although vertebrates number about 40,000 species, they account for only about 2 percent of all animals on earth. The remaining 98 percent consist of a wide variety of organisms, including INSECTS, sponges, and JELLYFISH.

Antartica ⚘ *See* CONTINENTS; POLAR REGIONS.

Ants ⚘ INSECTS that often live in colonies of hundreds or thousands of female workers headed by one queen, the only female that lays eggs. Ant colonies generally have only a few male ants, whose main job is to fertilize the queen.

Ants live throughout the world, except in the POLAR REGIONS and at very high ALTITUDES, or elevations. Most ant SPECIES live in the TROPICAL regions. Ants are important in their HABITAT because they eat other insects and help control insect populations, RECYCLE plant material, disperse SEEDS, and turn over SOIL.

Apes ⚘ Members of a group of MAMMALS called *primates*, which includes monkeys and humans. Apes are the closest living relatives to humans. The largest of the primates, apes have no tail, and their forelimbs are longer than their hind legs. The

Like most ants, leaf-cutting ants live in a complex social structure. They use the leaves they harvest to make a medium for the fungi they eat.

Apes, which include this gorilla, are the closest relatives to humans. In Africa, apes are threatened by habitat loss.

slender gibbons and the larger orangutan live in the TROPICAL FORESTS of Asia. These primates are arboreal, meaning that they live mostly in trees. Gibbons are spectacular acrobats, swinging with their long limbs from branch to branch. The chimpanzee and the gorilla of Africa are more terrestrial, spending more time on the ground but building their nighttime sleeping nests in trees.

Aquatic Environments ♣

Areas where water is the primary factor in the ENVIRONMENT and for the PLANTS and ANIMALS that live there. Aquatic environments may be fresh or salt water or a combination of the two, called *brackish*. The pelagic zone aquatic environment includes all the water in the oceans and is the largest of all the environments on Earth. Other aquatic environments may be inland—such as ponds, rivers, and BOGS—or they may be coastal, such as SWAMPS of MANGROVES and ESTUARIES. [*See also* FRESHWATER BIOMES; MARINE BIOMES.]

Arctic Ocean ♣ *See* OCEANS.

Asia ♣ *See* CONTINENTS.

Atlantic Ocean ♣ *See* OCEANS.

Atmosphere ♣ The mixture of gases that surrounds Earth. The major gases in Earth's atmosphere are nitrogen, OXYGEN, and carbon dioxide. The atmosphere also contains other gases, water vapor, and dust particles.

The atmosphere protects life on Earth from harmful radiation from the SUN. It also absorbs heat from the Sun, which protects the planet from becoming too hot or too cold.

Earth's atmosphere is made up of four layers. The TROPOSPHERE, the layer closest to the planet, extends up about 10 miles (16 kilometers) at the EQUATOR, about 8 miles (13 kilometers) in the Northern and Southern hemispheres, and only about 4 miles (6.4 kilometers) in the POLAR REGIONS. The troposphere is where the planet's weather is produced and most clouds occur. The second layer, called the *stratosphere*, is about 20 miles (32 kilometers) thick. In the lower stratosphere, the temperature is very cold. But midway up, the temperature becomes warm due to the OZONE layer, which protects Earth from the sun's ultraviolet radiation. The *mesosphere*, the layer of the atmosphere above the stratosphere, is very cold. The top layer, the *ionosphere*, is very thin and nearest to the sun. In this layer, ultraviolet radiation, X-rays, and showers of particles from the sun change molecules of gas into electrically charged particles, a process called *ionization*.

Australia ♣ *See* CONTINENTS.

Bacteria ☙ One-celled ORGANISMS that do not have a nucleus. Bacteria are the most common organisms on EARTH, living almost everywhere. Though they can cause diseases in PLANTS and ANIMALS, bacteria are extremely important in ECOSYSTEMS. Many bacteria exist in symbiosis with other organisms. Like FUNGI, many bacteria feed on dead and dying organisms, helping to recycle nutrients. The weathering of ROCKS, which releases important elements into the ATMOSPHERE and SOIL, is enhanced by certain bacteria. [*See also* NITROGEN CYCLE.]

Where are They Found? Bacteria on Mars

Bacteria can be found just about everywhere on EARTH—from the tops of MOUNTAINS to the depths of the OCEANS. Scientists at the University of Georgia have estimated that there are 5 million trillion bacteria on our planet.

Some scientists believe that there is life on Mars in the form of bacteria. Recent examinations by a powerful scanning electron microscope of a meteorite from Mars that fell in Egypt in 1911 revealed particles that are similar in size to bacteria found on Earth. Some researchers believe they may be fossilized bacterial colonies, but other scientists question whether these tiny structures are really evidence of living ORGANISMS on Mars.

Beavers ☙ Semiaquatic MAMMALS with brown fur; webbed hind feet; huge front teeth; and a scaly, flat, paddle-like tail. Beavers are nocturnal

Beavers eat a variety of tree barks and twigs. They also use sticks to build mound-shaped lodges and dams along streams.

and live in streams and lakes. They mostly eat the bark and twigs of trees.

Social animals that work and play together, beavers build mound-shaped lodges out of mud, grass, and sticks along the shoreline of lakes and streams. Beavers change AQUATIC ENVIRONMENTS by building dams out of sticks and logs to increase the area and depth of water around their lodges. Although the dams cause local flooding, they help control RUNOFF and create HABITATS for FISH, water-fowl, and other aquatic ANIMALS.

Beetles ⚘ INSECTS that have hardened front wings, which usually cover the beetle like a hard shell. Beetles range in size from less than .04 inches (0.1 centimeter) to the Hercules beetle, which can measure 6 inches (16 centimeters). There are more types of beetles than any other ANIMALS in the world. Estimates vary from 350,000 to 8 million SPECIES. Beetles live in many HABITATS and are found almost everywhere on EARTH. Some beetles are beneficial to humans. The ladybug, or ladybird, beetles are important in AGRICULTURE because they prey on other insect pests. Dung beetles literally live on waste material of other animals, helping to clean the ENVIRONMENT. Some beetles are PARASITES and live in the nests of ants or bees, eating the food that the host insects bring back to the nest. While some beetles are beneficial, many beetle species eat wood, flowers, and fruits of PLANTS, causing economic damage to farm crops. Partly because of their abundance, beetles play a major role in many ECOSYSTEMS.

Benthic ⚘ *See* MARINE BIOMES.

Biodegradable ⚘ A substance that is biodegradable is able to break down biologically into raw materials that become part of the ENVIRONMENT. Any natural product can biodegrade. A tree leaf, for example, eventually falls to the ground and decomposes, releasing nutrients into the SOIL that nourish the tree and other PLANTS for the next growing season. The word *biodegradable* is often used today to refer to plastics and other synthetic products that are able to break down when exposed to BACTERIA and other MICROORGANISMS.

Biodiversity ⚘ *See* BIOLOGICAL DIVERSITY.

Biogeography ⚘ The study of SPECIES distribution—that is, where PLANTS and ANIMALS live in a particular BIOME. In a TROPICAL FOREST, for example, some plants will be found living only in very high elevations, perhaps because rainfall is highest

there. Other plant species cannot live with that much rain and prefer the lower ALTITUDES in the same biome.

Biological Community ♣ Includes all the various SPECIES that live together in a common location. A FOREST community, for example, consists of all the trees and other PLANTS, the ANIMALS, FUNGI, BACTERIA, and other MICROORGANISMS in that ECOSYSTEM. Each member of a biological community possesses ADAPTATIONS that enable it to live there. Each member of the community also occupies its own NICHE and interacts with other members in a particular food web. Forest plants, for example, are eaten by deer and other HERBIVORES, which are, in turn, eaten by CARNIVORES. When the top PREDATOR dies, the bacteria and other organisms in the community aid in DECOMPOSITION, returning the nutrients to the ENVIRONMENT. [*See also* FOOD CHAINS AND WEBS.]

Biological Diversity ♣ Also called *biodiversity*, this refers to the variety of living ORGANISMS on EARTH. Approximately 1.5 million SPECIES of organisms have been named and described, and many more remain to be discovered. Organisms range from microscopic BACTERIA to the huge sequoia TREES of California to worm-like

creatures that live in OCEAN depths thousands of feet below the surface.

Biological diversity also refers to genetic differences among organisms of the same species. This is called *genetic diversity*. An example would be differences in eye color.

This great biological diversity of life has evolved over billions of years as PLANTS and ANIMALS adapted to the changes in the ENVIRONMENT. Earth has experienced great changes in temperature, sea level, and ATMOSPHERE throughout the planet's long history. Many species became extinct and others evolved. Most extinctions on Earth happened naturally. Today, however, human activities are causing so many changes in the environment so quickly that they endanger species and ECOSYSTEMS, resulting in the loss of biological diversity.

Biomes ♣ Geographic regions that share similar characteristics, especially CLIMATE and types of PLANTS and ANIMALS. Each biome may contain many different ECOSYSTEMS.

DESERTS, for example, are all considered part of the same biome, mainly because they are all dry. That does not mean that all deserts are the same, however. Some deserts are hot while others are cold. Some deserts are rocky while others are sandy. Because deserts are very dry, all deserts

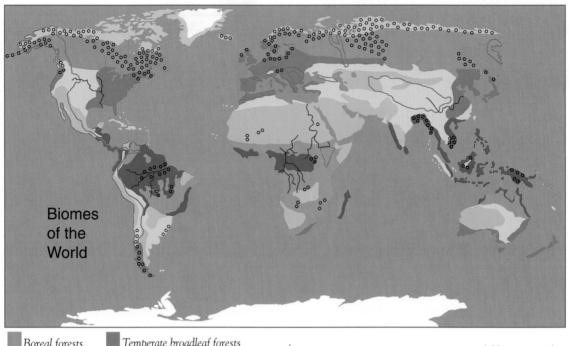

Biomes of the World

▮ Boreal forests	▮ Temperate broadleaf forests
▮ Deserts	▮ Temperate grasslands
▮ Freshwater biomes	▮ Tropical forests
▮ Marine biomes	▮ Tropical grasslands
▯ Mountains	▮ Tundra
▯ Polar regions	⁰ᵒ°ₒ Wetlands

are home to certain plants and animals that do not need much water to survive. Among the types of ORGANISMS common to many deserts are cacti, scorpions, and REPTILES.

TEMPERATE GRASSLANDS and TROPICAL GRASSLANDS are also dry biomes, but not as dry as deserts. These biomes can be recognized by vast plains of GRASSES and by the grazing animals that feed on them, such as antelope, BISON, or kangaroos.

There are three basic types of forest biomes: BOREAL FORESTS, TROPICAL FORESTS, and TEMPERATE BROADLEAF FORESTS. All contain TREES AND SHRUBS as well as various animals especially suited for forest life, such as squirrels, various types of BIRDS, and perhaps monkeys or APES.

Far to the north lies a cold, treeless biome called the TUNDRA, which is home to a more limited number of plants and animals, including the shaggy-coated musk ox and the caribou. At the extreme north and south of the earth are the ice-covered POLAR REGIONS. Animals like penguins and polar bears survive well on the ice of these areas.

Biosphere ♣ The zone of the EARTH that supports life, extending from the deepest depths of the OCEANS to the upper ATMOSPHERE. The biosphere is a global ECOSYSTEM, the largest possible BIOLOGICAL COMMUNITY. It can be divided into regions that have similar climatic conditions called BIOMES. Biomes can be further divided into ECOSYSTEMS, while each ecosystem contains a number of smaller biological communities. The biosphere is made up of all the living ORGANISMS and the nonliving things that provide the energy and nutrients needed to support life on Earth.

Biotechnology ⚘

The application of new techniques and instruments in the biological sciences. Discoveries in biotechnology have led to the development of crops that have greater resistance to INSECT pests. They have also enabled farmers to grow more and better food on less land. Much of the research in biotechnology is linked to the development of GENETIC ENGINEERING. Future applications of biotechnology may include the development of alternative ENERGY SOURCES that will reduce human dependence on non-renewable resources. Biotechnology is not without potential drawbacks. The use of genetically engineered crops in human food has raised controversy over whether eating those foods could harm people.

Birds ⚘

The only ANIMALS with feathers. Birds also have wings, but so do

Birds play an important role in ecosystems. This bird is a mute swan.

bats and INSECTS. Nearly all birds can use their wings to fly, but a few, such as the ostrich of Africa, the rhea of South America, and the penguin, do not fly. There are more than 9,000 SPECIES of birds. They come in all shapes, sizes, and colors and live in all kinds of HABITATS.

Birds are WARM-BLOODED like MAMMALS, but they develop from eggs laid by the female, as REPTILES do. Many species of birds migrate with the SEASONS, flying south when fall arrives in the Northern Hemisphere, and then heading north in the spring.

Birds play important roles in their ECOSYSTEMS. Predatory birds eat insects and rodents. Birds serve as food for humans and other animals. They also indicate the health of the ENVIRONMENT. For example, the disappearance of bald eagles in North

(continues on p. 18)

Boreal Forests

Boreal Forests Also called the *taiga*. Boreal forests are made up of coniferous trees, also known as conifers, that can survive extremely cold winter weather. The conelike shape of conifers helps them stand up without breaking under heavy snowfalls. The SOIL under the boreal forest is poor, being high in acid content and low in minerals such as calcium, magnesium, and potassium. Boreal forests close to the TUNDRA have a layer of permanently frozen soil called PERMAFROST.

Regions and Climate. Boreal forests are found in Canada and Siberia in Russia. They form a ring between the tundra to the north and the TEMPERATE BROADLEAF FORESTS to the south.

The climate of boreal forests is seasonal, with long, very cold winters and short summers. PRECIPITATION falls mainly as snow, but there are also heavy summer rains.

Plants. Boreal forest PLANTS tend to be relatively short. There are not very many kinds of plants, mostly because of the poor soils. Conifers such as spruces, firs, and pines dominate this biome. White spruce and balsam fir are common in eastern boreal forests. Black spruce, white cedars, and tamaracks are found in wet areas. Boreal forests are often damaged by a moth called the spruce budworm, which eats fir and spruce needles and can kill entire trees. Some broadleaf trees, such as aspen and alder, are also found in boreal forests. There is not much underbrush in boreal forests. LICHENS, MOSSES, and FERNS grow on the forest floor, along with cherries, blueberries, and short dogwood trees.

Animals. Only a few SNAKES and AMPHIBIANS can tolerate the cold con-

Biome Snapshot: Boreal Forests

Geographical Regions: North of the TEMPERATE BROADLEAF FORESTS of North America, Europe, and Asia, in the country of Canada, and in the region of Siberia in Russia; bordered on the north by tundra biomes. **Climate:** Cold winters and cool summers; range of temperatures from 5 to -40°F (-15 to -40°C) and from 50 to 59°F (10 to 15°C). **Precipitation:** Low, only 15 to 40 inches (40 to 100 cm) per year, mainly in the form of heavy winter snows and summer rains. **Seasons:** Long, cold winters with summers lasting only about 120 days. **Dominant Plant Life:** Coniferous trees, lichens, ferns, and berries. **Dominant Animal Life:** Lynx, caribou, deer, moose, elk, bears; mice, squirrels, hares, foxes, and beavers; jays, nuthatches, chickadees, and warblers.

ditions found in boreal forests. The common garter snake is one of the few REPTILES found throughout much of the boreal forest biome. Amphibians such as the boreal chorus frog, American toad, and wood frog are found in many areas. The boreal forest is almost the only place where mink frogs are found. INSECTS are abundant only in those seasons when conditions are more moderate. The BIRDS of the boreal forest include jays, nuthatches, chickadees, and wood warblers. MAMMALS, with their thick coats of fur, also are common. Mice, squirrels, hares, foxes, and beavers are familiar boreal forest mammals. Larger mammals

Coniferous trees are the dominant plant family within boreal forests. These trees, many of which keep their needles year round, can survive cold, harsh winters.

Key Species: Larch

American larch trees, also called *tamaracks*, are a type of conifer found in forests ranging from northern Pennsyvania and Illinois north into the boreal forests of Canada. A close relative, the European larch, is found in central and western Europe. Larches grow in the boreal forests of Siberia.

Most conifers are evergreen. Larch conifers are curious because each fall their leaves turn from green to yellow and are shed just like the leaves of broadleafed trees. The wood of larches is used as poles and for construction. The bark contains chemicals called *tannins*, which are used to make leather.

typically found there include lynx, grizzly bears, timber wolves, moose, elk, caribou, white-tailed deer, and mule deer.

Human Impact. The greatest danger to boreal forests is overharvesting of lumber, which can cause long-lasting damage to the forests while also destroying HABITATS for many ENDANGERED AND THREATENED SPECIES. AIR POLLUTION in the form of ACID RAIN threatens the health of boreal forest trees. In addition, many tracts of boreal forest are flooded and lost when rivers are dammed. [*See also* TREES AND SHRUBS.]

Where Are They Found? Chilling Out

BIRDS are found in every region on Earth, even in the POLAR REGIONS. Most birds that live in these cold areas do so only during the short summer months, because it is difficult to find food in the winter. Many geese and shorebirds migrate to the Arctic, where they breed, lay their eggs, and raise their young. Then, in the fall, they head to warmer areas for the winter.

One SPECIES of bird, the emperor penguin, spends its entire life in icy cold Antarctica. The emperor eats small fish that live in the cold antarctic waters. Emperor penguins lay their eggs in winter. The adults huddle together in large groups and incubate the eggs on their feet and under a pouch of belly skin to keep them off the ice and warm.

(continued from p. 15)
America in the mid-1900s brought attention to the harmful effects of DDT and other PESTICIDES.

Bison ♣ A large, brown, oxlike MAMMAL. The American bison, commonly known as the buffalo, once numbered perhaps 50 million. By grazing on GRASSLANDS, the bison helped to maintain the grassland ECOSYSTEM in North America.

The Plains Indians depended on the bison for its meat, used the hides and fur for clothing and shelter, and made tools from the bones and horns. The introduction of horses to the Indians and the extension of railroads across the United States led to the killing of the huge bison herds.

By 1889, bison were facing extinction, with fewer than 1,000 left in the United States. Action by various CONSERVATION ORGANIZATIONS ensured the survival of the remaining animals. Today there are about 350,000 bison in the United States.

Bog ♣ A type of WETLAND characterized by evergreen TREES AND SHRUBS, where the ground is covered with a thick carpet of sphagnum MOSS. Bogs are highly acidic and poor in nutrients, so DECOMPOSITION takes place very slowly. Decomposed PLANT material accumulates and forms a spongy layer called *peat*, which is often harvested to provide heat.

Since bogs decompose slowly, they serve as a type of time capsule, providing clues to what the vegetation and climate in a particular region was like centuries ago.

A variety of AMPHIBIANS live in bogs. In Europe, peat has been harvested from bogs to provide heat, and many peatlands have become endangered ECOSYSTEMS.

Carbon Cycle
Movement of carbon within an ECOSYSTEM. In the chemistry of life, carbon is the building block upon which all ORGANISMS are constructed. Through the process of PHOTOSYNTHESIS, PLANTS convert carbon dioxide gas found in the ATMOSPHERE or dissolved in water into various nutrients. These nutrients in turn provide food and energy for humans and other ANIMALS, FUNGI, BACTERIA, and other microscopic organisms. As this food is broken down and used by cells, carbon dioxide gas is released back into the atmosphere. When animals and other living things die, the carbon compounds in cells are broken down through DECOMPOSITION and returned to the ENVIRONMENT to be reused by plants. In the carbon cycle, plants also release OXYGEN into the atmosphere during photosynthesis.

Carbon dioxide helps regulate temperatures on the EARTH by absorbing some of the heat from the sun. The release of additional carbon dioxide produced by industry and AGRICULTURE into the atmosphere may contribute to a condition known as the GREENHOUSE EFFECT, which may lead to changes in the CLIMATE. Such changes, even small ones, could cause rapid melting of polar ice, resulting in a rise in sea level and flooding of COASTLINES. Climate change caused by the greenhouse effect could affect humans, animals, and even entire ecosystems. [*See also* NUTRIENT CYCLE.]

Carbon Dioxide
See CARBON CYCLE.

Carnivores
ANIMALS that usually feed on meat. An important part of most food webs, carnivores feed on HERBIVORES, which in turn feed on PLANTS and small ORGANISMS. Some plants are carnivorous and trap INSECTS for food. Among these are the pitcher plants.

Carnivore also refers to a scientific classification of animals that have

The grizzly bear is one of the largest and most feared carnivores. In addition to eating meat, grizzly bears are also omnivores, which means they eat berries and other plant parts as well.

canine teeth and claws (such as lions, tigers, and bears). [*See also* FOOD CHAINS AND WEBS; PREDATORS.]

Caves ☙ Naturally formed chambers beneath the surface of the EARTH or in the sides of hills, cliffs, or MOUNTAINS. A cave may consist of many underground chambers connected by small passageways to form a cave system. For example, Mammoth Cave National Park in Kentucky has a number of layers of underground chambers with a subterranean stream at the lowest level.

Caves form mainly as a result of water breaking down SOIL and ROCK, particularly limestone. Carbon dioxide and other compounds in water dissolve the limestone and carry it away. Some caves may be formed by ocean wave action along the COASTLINES. Other types of caves include lava caves, which form under lava flows from VOLCANOES; and ice caves, which form in GLACIERS and icebergs.

PLANTS and ANIMALS that inhabit caves and underground chambers have evolved special ADAPTATIONS that enable them to live there. Cave crickets and cave FISH, for example, are usually blind but have highly developed senses of touch. FUNGI are the only plants that can grow inside caves. The groundwater in the caves contains nutrients that support the fungi.

A series of limestone caves, Carlsbad Caverns in New Mexico provide a habitat for thousands of bats and various cave-dwelling organisms.

Many cave-dwelling ORGANISMS live near the cave entrance, where some light penetrates and they can leave to forage for food. Many species of bats rest and hibernate in caves, but find their food outside. Rich deposits of bat droppings, called *guano*, build up in caves over many years. The guano provides food for various species of INSECTS and other INVERTEBRATES. The Texas blind salamander specializes in eating invertebrates that feed on the guano. In some countries, people use the guano as fertilizer.

Chaparral & *See* SCRUBLANDS.

Chemosynthesis & A process in which ORGANISMS produce their own organic substances from inorganic compounds. For example, certain BACTERIA living in caves use hydrogen sulfide that they take from the air to make carbohydrates as food. Spiders and scorpions feed on other INVERTEBRATES that live deep in the cave and eat the bacteria. This is an example of an ECOSYSTEM that depends on chemosynthesis rather than PHOTOSYNTHESIS for energy.

Chlorofluorocarbons (CFCs)
& Chemical compounds released into the ATMOSPHERE that contain carbon, chlorine, fluorine, and sometimes hydrogen. They are used in refrigeration, cleaning materials, aerosol cans, and plastic foams. Commonly called CFCs, chlorofluorocarbons are suspected to be a major cause of the depletion of the OZONE layer that protects the EARTH from the sun's harmful rays.

During the 1970s, scientists discovered a hole in the ozone layer over Antarctica and that chlorofluorocarbons were a major cause. To halt destruction of the protective ozone, the United States banned the use of chlorofluorocarbons in 1978. In 1987, a number of countries signed the Montreal Protocol, which called for an end to CFC production. Although the manufacture and use of new CFCs have been prohibited in a number of developed countries, CFCs remain a problem, and the threat to the ozone layer still exists.

Clearcutting & *See* LOGGING.

Climate and Weather & Atmospheric conditions in a region. Weather refers to the air temperature, PRECIPITATION, WIND, humidity, and amount of sunlight on a particular day. For example, on a given day an area may experience sunny, cloudy, or partly cloudy conditions, and it may be windy and dry. Weather varies from day to day and can be unpredictable.

An area's climate is the average, or usual, weather conditions for a

Atmospheric weather conditions are capable of producing powerful disturbances, such as this dangerous bolt of lightning.

region over a whole year. More predictable, climate is a combination of air temperature, rainfall, wind, and humidity. An area's climate is determined by how much heat it receives from the SUN; by wind patterns, or air currents; and by average precipitation. EVAPORATION, driven by wind and the water vapor in the air, determines how dry a region will be.

Climate and weather, especially air temperature and rainfall, are important in determining which PLANTS, ANIMALS, and other ORGANISMS live in different parts of the world. Plants are especially dependent on annual rainfalls. For example, trees found in TEMPERATE regions need 46 to 56 inches (115 to 140 centimeters) of precipitation each year, whereas conifer trees can survive with just 30 inches (75 centimeters) of rain. GRASSES grow in areas with precipitation of less than 10 inches (25 centimeters). Cacti are found in areas with 2 to 4 inches (5 to 10 centimeters) of rainfall.

TROPICAL regions, which are near the EQUATOR, receive more sunlight than other parts of the Earth. Tropical BIOMES experience constant warm weather, high rainfall, and little or no seasonal weather changes. Most trees found in tropical biomes cannot tolerate colder conditions.

POLAR REGIONS and the TUNDRA receive much less sunlight and, as a result, have cold, harsh climates. These regions have the longest and coldest winters. The higher elevations of MOUNTAINS also have cold, harsh climates. The trees found in these places are conifers, trees that are adapted to withstand long, cold winters.

TEMPERATE zones have more seasonal climates that can vary from cold, snowy winters to hot, rainy summers. Trees found in temperate biomes are usually broadleafed SPECIES that drop their leaves in the fall. [See also WATER CYCLE.]

Climate Change ☙ The effect of natural processes and human activities on EARTH'S ATMOSPHERE. Among the natural processes that can affect climate are ICE AGES and long-term

volcanic activity. During the ice ages, large areas of the earth were covered by vast ice sheets. The presence of the ice cooled the CLIMATE in many places on Earth. Volcanic activity can also cause climate change, usually on a short-term basis. The gases and dust released by erupting VOLCANOES can block out the rays of the SUN, resulting in a cooling effect on the climate.

Human activities can have a significant effect on climate. Humans release carbon dioxide and other gases into the air at rates much faster than the planet can cycle them. As the levels of these gases in the atmosphere increase, the gases trap the sun's heat and raise the temperature of the earth, causing a general warming called the GREENHOUSE EFFECT. Each year, humans burn billions of tons of fossil fuels, such as coal and oil. The gases produced by these burning fuels do not disappear immediately or even over the course of a year. The gases that are released today will likely be affecting the climate well into the future.

Continued warming of the climate may result in melting of the polar ice caps, raising the levels of the OCEANS, causing flooding and EROSION along COASTLINES. Higher temperatures can affect AGRICULTURE, producing less food for livestock and people.

These changes may also affect entire ECOSYSTEMS. For example, PLANTS and ANIMALS that have evolved ADAPTATIONS to live in certain BIOMES may not be able to survive there if the climate changes significantly. The loss of PLANTS, which take in carbon dioxide during PHOTOSYNTHESIS, will result in even more climate change.

Climate change is a complex issue. Not everyone agrees that it is occurring or that the long-term impacts will be harmful. Governments and experts continue to debate the issue and what effect it will have on life on Earth.

Climax Species ⚘

The ORGANISMS that typically live in a mature BIOLOGICAL COMMUNITY, which is in the final stage of SUCCESSION. Climax species are often large TREES and other PLANTS that have long life cycles. The biodiversity of climax communities is often high, and these species are able to resist minor changes in the ECOSYSTEM. Beech and maple trees are examples of climax species in a TEMPERATE BROADLEAF FOREST. Climax species are not permanent in the community, however, because disturbances such as FIRE and extreme drought can cause vast changes in the ENVIRONMENT. Climax communities often change over time.

Cloud Forest ⚘

An area of mountainous forest that receives water not only from rain but also from dense banks of fog. The TREES in a cloud forest are usually short and crooked. MOSSES, climbing FERNS, LICHENS, and orchids obtain water from the fog and grow in abundance, covering tree trunks and branches as well as the ground. The moist cloud forest is also home to a rich variety of AMPHIBIANS. A cloud forest of extremely short, moss-covered trees is sometimes known as an *elfin woodland*. Cloud forests are very important because they act like sponges, soaking up moisture and releasing it slowly back into the ATMOSPHERE.

Clouds and Fog ♠ Visible masses

of water droplets and ice crystals suspended in the air. A shallow layer of cloud at or near ground level is called fog.

Clouds and fog are both formed from water droplets or ice crystals suspended in the air.

Clouds typically form when moist air rises. As the air rises, it expands and becomes cool and supermoist. The excess water vapor in the air condenses—changes from a gas to a liquid—and collects around dust or smoke particles, forming droplets and ice crystals.

Meteorologists classify clouds primarily by their ALTITUDE and appearance. High, feathery-looking clouds are *cirrus* clouds. Puffy, white clouds are *cumulus* clouds.

Coastlines ♠ The areas of land that

border the EARTH'S OCEANS. They are also called *shorelines*. There are about 193,000 miles (312,000 kilometers) of

The earth's coastlines include sandy beaches and rocky shores, which provide diverse habitats for a variety of plants and animals.

coastlines that run along the CONTINENTS of world.

Coastlines contain diverse HABITATS that sustain a variety of PLANTS and ANIMALS. For example, rocky coasts along the United States provide rough surfaces on which barnacles and periwinkles (a type of snail) can attach themselves. Ocean waves roll over these animals and bring them tiny ORGANISMS to eat. The barnacles in turn are eaten by starfish, FISH, and BIRDS called oystercatchers. Sandy coastlines provide habitats for other types of plants and animals.

Cold-blooded ⚘ A term referring to ANIMALS with body temperatures that vary with the temperature of their ENVIRONMENT. Cold-bloodedness is also called *poikilothermy* or *ectothermy*.

Commensalism ⚘ *See* MUTUALISM.

Coniferous ⚘ *See* PLANTS; TREES AND SHRUBS.

Conservation ⚘ The protection and preservation of wild PLANTS and ANIMALS and their HABITATS. Conservation includes protection of ENDANGERED AND THREATENED SPECIES, careful use and RECYCLING of mineral resources, and careful use of products such as fossil fuels and lumber to

ensure their current and future availability.

In the United States, support for conservation began to emerge in the mid-1800s. President Theodore Roosevelt was among those who first advocated the establishment of Yellowstone National Park in 1872 to protect that ECOSYSTEM. However, enforcement of conservation measures did not come about until the U.S. Endangered Species Act of 1969 and the Convention on International Trade in Endangered Species (CITES) of 1973. Both of these measures regulate the importation and exportation of rare, threatened, and endangered species.

There are many different conservation efforts going on in the world today. One of the most well-known wildlife conservation efforts today centers on saving the bamboo forest habitat of western China's giant panda and ensuring the future of that SPECIES through breeding in captivity. Protecting the world's TROPICAL FORESTS—which help regulate the amount of moisture in the ATMOSPHERE and probably contain more BIOLOGICAL DIVERSITY than any other BIOME—is another major conservation effort.

Conservation Organizations
⚘ Groups of people united in working toward protection of the world's

PLANTS, ANIMALS, and NATURAL RESOURCES. The World Conservation Union (IUCN), which was created in 1948, is the world's largest conservation organization. Its headquarters are in Switzerland, and it brings together 76 countries and some 10,000 scientists and experts.

There are many conservation organizations in the United States. Among the oldest are the Sierra Club, founded in 1892, and the Wildlife Conservation Society, established in 1895.

Consumer ☙ When applied to humans, the term refers to people who buy and use either raw materials or finished products, such as gasoline, soap, or automobiles. Consumers can determine the effect that industry has on the ENVIRONMENT by choosing to buy goods that are safe and non-polluting.

Consumers also refers to PLANTS and ANIMALS that obtain food by preying on other ORGANISMS or by eating particles of organic matter. Unlike PRODUCERS, consumers generally do not make their own food.

Continental Drift ☙ *See* PLATE TECTONICS.

Continents ☙ EARTH's major land masses. The six continents are Africa; Antarctica; Australasia, which includes Australia and New Guinea; Eurasia, which includes Europe, China, and India; North America; and South America. The boundaries of the continents are not their COASTLINES but an edge that generally lies several hundred miles offshore, where the slope of the continental shelf—a broad, relatively shallow underwater platform that typically extends from the coast to depths of 330 to 660 feet (100 to 200 meters)—drops off abruptly to much greater depths.

Convergence ☙ The EVOLUTION of similar characteristics, such as body structures or behavioral traits, among unrelated ORGANISMS. For example, SHARKS and dolphins evolved as fast, torpedo-shaped swimmers in AQUATIC ENVIRONMENTS. The wings of bats, BIRDS, and INSECTS can also be considered convergence. Convergent evolution often occurs because NATURAL SELECTION frequently favors similar ADAPTATIONS among organisms that share similar physical environments.

PLANTS also display convergence. The cacti of the New World and the plants in Africa called euphorbias are not closely related, but they look similar and are well adapted to living in DESERT HABITATS.

Coral Reefs ☙ Structures found in shallow, warm parts of the OCEANS

and formed by the external skeletons of marine INVERTEBRATES called *coral polyps*. While alive, these ANIMALS divide and grow into large colonies that are attached to the sea floor. The hard skeletons of the coral polyps form the basic structure of the reef. Coral reefs form underwater and above-water HABITATS for flowering PLANTS, sea grasses, and small FISH, which are eaten by larger fish and marine MAMMALS.

As material accumulates on the reef, it may rise above the water's surface, forming a coral island with sandy DUNES and beaches. Many South Pacific ISLANDS began as coral reefs. Other reef systems are raised

Coral reefs are made up of external skeletons of millions of tiny organisms. Many colorful fish, as well as various other creatures, are found there.

above sea level by movements of the Earth's crust. Coral islands of this type, such as the Aldabra Islands in the Indian Ocean, often have rocky plateaus with cliffs.

Coriolis Force
The tendency of a moving body, such as air or OCEAN CURRENTS, to drift to the right in the Northern Hemisphere and to the left in the Southern Hemisphere. This directional movement is a result of Earth's rotation around its axis, in which the surface of the planet rotates at a faster speed near the equator than it does near the poles. The Coriolis force strongly influences wind systems and ocean currents such as the Gulf Stream, a major Atlantic Ocean current system.

Crustaceans
Group of INVERTEBRATES called *arthropods* that include crabs, lobsters, and shrimps. All arthropods have hard external skeletons and jointed legs. Crustaceans occupy almost every NICHE within EARTH'S AQUATIC ENVIRONMENTS. Extremely small SPECIES of arthropods form part of the PLANKTON found in lakes and OCEANS. Other arthropods, such as crabs, live at the bottom of the sea. Isopods, commonly called *pill bugs*, are among the few crustaceans that live on land. Crustaceans are valuable sources of food for humans as well as other ANIMALS.

Day Length

Day Length ⚘ The amount of time between sunrise and sunset. The amount of daylight varies depending on location on earth and the season of the year. Day length has a great influence on PLANTS and ANIMALS as a result of the seasonal distribution of sunlight. For example, many SPECIES of BIRDS, such as the red knot, respond to a shortening of day length by migrating from northern breeding grounds to southern regions, where food is more plentiful during the winter.

Deciduous ⚘ *See* PLANTS; TREES AND SHRUBS.

Decomposition ⚘ A chemical process in which organic matter is broken down into simple materials. When a PLANT or ANIMAL dies, it is fed on by organisms such as BEETLES, BACTERIA, and FUNGI. This is one way nutrients are recycled in an ECO-SYSTEM.

All organic material eventually decomposes. The rate at which an or-ganism decomposes varies with its chemical composition, the amount of surface area exposed to light, the amount of OXYGEN and moisture in the air, and the air temperature.

Decomposition can help clean up the ENVIRONMENT. Certain bacteria, for example, can be used to break down oil spills into organic materials that are recycled into the environment. [*See also* NUTRIENT CYCLE; WATER POLLUTION.]

Deforestation ⚘ *See* LOGGING.

Desertification ⚘ The spread of a DESERT environment into areas that were not previously desert. Desertification is usually caused by CLIMATE CHANGE, by human activities, or both. A temporary severe drought, or prolonged decrease in rain, may cause a region to become desertified. Among the human causes of desertification are the removal of natural vegetation, which results in high levels of EROSION; OVERGRAZING by livestock; and using up surface or ground water

In some parts of the world, deserts are expanding into new areas in a process known as *desertification.*

supplies for irrigation, industry, and households. Desertification reduces BIOLOGICAL DIVERSITY and the productivity of ECOSYSTEMS.

Desertification is not a new phenomenon. About 7,000 years ago, parts of North Africa contained FORESTS and fertile land for AGRICULTURE. Today, much of that region is desert.

Deserts ♣ *See* page 30.

Development ♣ The creation of new homes, industrial areas, and grazing and farm lands. HABITAT LOSS caused by development is a leading factor in the decline of many SPECIES of PLANTS and ANIMALS. In some cases, habitat alteration may be large-scale: the creation of a pineapple plantation requires cutting down large areas of TROPICAL FOREST. In other instances, wildlife habitat is gradually changed, as when a native GRASSLAND is slowly replaced by houses in a suburban development.

Diversity ♣ *See* BIOLOGICAL DIVERSITY.

Drinking Water ♣ Living ORGANISMS need this to replenish the water in the body. The human body is more than three-quarters water. Water *(continues on p. 32)*

Some areas of the world, such as parts of India, face severe shortages of good drinking water.

Deserts ⚜ Dry regions with very low yearly rainfall and high EVAPORATION rates. Cold deserts, such as the TUNDRA and POLAR REGIONS, receive their PRECIPITATION as snow. Hot deserts are known for their sand, bare ROCKS, and general lack of TREES. These deserts experience dust storms and sand storms, and may have sudden, violent rain showers.

Regions. The world's hot deserts are found mostly between latitudes 15° and 30° north and south. The largest hot desert in the world is the Sahara desert of northern Africa. North American deserts include the

Deserts are not just sand. Many desert areas also contain a variety of animal and plant life, including cactus plants.

very hot deserts of the American southwest and the colder deserts of the Great Basin region.

Climate. Most hot deserts have hot days and cold nights. Daytime temperatures can reach over 100°F (38°C), while at night there can be frost. Most deserts are very dry, with less than 10 inches (25 centimeters) of rain per year. The ground is so dry and hard that sudden rains can cause flash floods.

Plants. Some deserts have woody shrubs—such as sagebrush, creosote bushes, and mesquite—and various succulents (plants like cacti that store water in their bodies). Cacti do not have leaves but they do have green stems used for PHOTOSYNTHESIS. A

Key Species: Scorpions

Scorpions are *arachnids* like spiders and mites. A scorpion has a long tail with a stinger that injects venom into prey. Scorpions are wonderfully adapted to dry conditions and are often the dominant PREDATOR in deserts. They are secretive, and hide in burrows or under objects during the day. Scorpions feed on insects and spiders at night. Some are large enough to eat lizards. Desert scorpions detect prey by noticing sand movements with sensors in their legs. A scorpion can find a cockroach 20 inches (50 centimeters) away and reach it with a few quick moves. Scorpions also perform complex mating dances. Young scorpions often ride on their mother's back when they are small.

waxy covering on the outside of cacti helps prevent water loss. These PLANTS also have prickly thorns that keep thirsty animals from biting into cacti for a drink.

Deserts are also home to small, short-lived flowering plants that come up and bloom only when it rains. Some desert plants have deep ROOTS up to 100 feet (23 meters) long that reach down to the WATER TABLE, which is often below the surface of the ground.

Animals. Deserts are home to various ANIMALS that have adapted to heat and dry conditions. Small animals avoid harsh conditions by living in burrows or by being active at night. Some animals, such as the kangaroo rat and the chuckwalla, never drink water.

INSECTS, spiders, and scorpions are common in the desert. There also are many lizards, SNAKES, and toads. Cactus wrens, roadrunners, and burrowing owls are just a few of the many desert BIRDS. Small MAMMALS include bats, rabbits, and squirrels.

Human Impact. Some of the world's deserts are growing larger. OVERGRAZING, deforestation, poor farming, and drought have resulted in DESERTIFICATION, or a change of GRASSLANDS and FORESTS into deserts. In 1882, only 9.4 percent of the Earth's surface was desert. Recent studies indicate that about 33 percent of the Earth's surface is now desert.

Biome Snapshot: Deserts

Geographical Region: Mostly between latitudes 15° and 30° north and south; major deserts found in northern and southern Africa, the Arabian Peninsula, Mongolia, and Argentina; Australia and North America also have deserts. **Altitude:** Varies; Death Valley, California is 282 feet (86 meters) below sea level; sand dunes in Sahara Desert reach almost 1,600 feet (488 meters) high. **Climate:** Cool, sometimes below freezing, at night; daytime temperatures over 100°F (38°C); average yearly temperatures from 75°F (24°C) to 86°F (30°C); generally dry conditions with sudden, heavy rainfall and flash floods. **Precipitation:** Less than 10 inches (25 centimeters) per year; parts of the Atacama desert in Chile have had no rain for at least 50 years. **Soils:** May be sandy, salty, or very rocky. **Dominant Plant Life:** Succulents such as cacti, thorny shrubs such as mesquite, and many annual plants. **Dominant Animal Life:** Many invertebrates, including insects, spiders, and scorpions; many lizards, snakes, and toads; cactus wrens and burrowing owls; kangaroo rats and other small mammals; mule deer.

Mining, irrigation, and dam building add to the destruction of desert HABITATS. Off-road vehicles crush plants, scare animals, and damage local TOPOGRAPHY.

(continued from p. 29)

covers 70 percent of the Earth's surface, but the majority of that water is salty and undrinkable or locked in ice in the POLAR REGIONS.

Many people obtain their drinking water from private and public wells. GROUNDWATER in aquifers is replenished by rainwater that seeps from the surface through the SOIL. This filtering process helps to purify the water. Wells are dug through the soil to reach the water reserves in the aquifers. Large towns and cities often build reservoirs that collect and provide water to residents. This water must be treated to make sure it is free from harmful chemicals, pollutants, and ORGANISMS that cause diseases, such as BACTERIA. Some communities recycle used water through sewage treatment plants, which remove harmful wastes, bacteria, and bad odors.

In areas where there is little available fresh groundwater, scientists have developed methods of taking the salt out of seawater. This process is called *desalinization*. However, fresh drinking water is scarce in many areas and remains an important environmental concern.

POLLUTION from pesticides and fertilizers, industrial wastes, and EROSION can affect the purity of drinking water. Industries in the United States are required to treat their wastewater before dumping it.

Most important of all, drinking water is a precious NATURAL RESOURCE, and there is a limited supply. It should not be wasted.

Dunes ☙ Hills or mounds of loose, fine-grained material, such as sand, that are heaped up and shaped by the wind. Dunes are found in DESERTS and along COASTLINES.

Dunes form when sand blown by the WIND catches on PLANTS or ROCKS. Dunes grow partly because they slow the wind, causing more sand to drop. Some of the tallest dunes in the world, found in the Sahara and the Namib deserts in Africa, are over 650 feet (200 meters) high.

Dunes are home to a number of SPECIES of plants and ANIMALS specifically adapted to the shifting sand. The web-footed gecko, for example, is a lizard that lives in the dunes of Africa's Namib Desert. Its webbed feet act like snowshoes, helping it to walk in the loose sand.

Earth

Earth ⚘ The third planet from the SUN. Earth is the only planet known to have living ORGANISMS. It gets just the right amount of sunlight to support life. Earth's water and ATMOSPHERE also support and protect living creatures. The Earth contains many different ECOSYSTEMS and BIOMES, which provide HABITATS for the various organisms that exist on the planet. [*See also* PLATE TECTONICS.]

Beautiful as seen from space, our Earth is the only planet in the solar system known to support life.

Earthquakes ⚘ Movements in the EARTH'S crust, or surface, that occur when underground ROCKS shift or break apart. Earthquakes tend to occur when large blocks of the Earth's crust called *tectonic plates* move against each other, causing pressure, or stress, to build up in the underlying rocks. When the rocks give way, energy in the form of seismic waves travels to the surface and causes a jolt or tremor that makes the land shake or tremble. Each earthquake is a reminder of the tremendous forces that shape the Earth. [*See also* PLATE TECTONICS; VOLCANOES.]

Ecology ⚘ The study of the relationships, or interactions, between ORGANISMS and their ENVIRONMENTS. Ecology explores the many ways in which an organism's life is shaped by other living organisms and abiotic factors, or non-living elements of the environment. It also looks at how POPULATIONS adapt to their surroundings and how different SPECIES live with one another. [*See also* ADAPTATION; EVOLUTION AND EXTINCTION; HABITAT.]

Ecoregion ⚘ Areas of the world

that have been subdivided into major HABITAT zones with similar CLIMATE AND WEATHER, physical features, and PLANTS and ANIMALS. Ecoregions help define the habitats and BIOLOGICAL DIVERSITY within a larger BIOME.

Ecosystem ⚘ All the living ORGAN-

ISMS in an area and the nonliving elements of their ENVIRONMENT such as SOIL and ROCKS. Ecosystems can be as small as a puddle or as large as an ocean. An ecosystem is notable for the complex ways its organisms are connected to one another and the environment through FOOD CHAINS AND WEBS and NUTRIENT CYCLES. Ecosys-

tems can change over time. For example, ponds sometimes dry up, and when this happens the pond may change into a BOG or MARSH ecosystem, which supports different organisms. [*See also* BIOME; SUCCESSION.]

Ecotourism ⚘ A type of travel that

focuses on a region's natural ENVIRONMENT and wildlife and attempts to leave them as undisturbed as possible. Ecotourism may include activities such as hiking, birdwatching, scuba diving, and wildlife photography.

Elephant ⚘ The heaviest of living

land MAMMALS. There are two elephant SPECIES. Both are found in TROPICAL HABITATS, and both are endangered. The Asian elephant lives mainly in India. It has small ears and a rounded forehead. This species has

These African elephants are herd animals that often live in close-knit groups. Wild elephants are found only in parts of Africa and Asia.

been trained to do heavy work for humans. The African elephant lives in tropical regions and savannas of Africa south of the Sahara Desert. This species is larger and has bigger tusks and ears than the Asian species.

In the wild, elephants live in close-knit social groups led by the oldest female. They often travel in larger groups of up to 100 animals. Hungry elephants dig up and destroy TREES AND SHRUBS, and can cause a great deal of damage to the ENVIRONMENT. [*See also* ENDANGERED AND THREATENED SPECIES.]

El Niño ♣ A large, warm OCEAN CURRENT that appears near the coast of Peru in South America every two to seven years. It causes a temporary CLIMATE CHANGE felt worldwide.

In a normal year with no El Niño, cool waters rich in nutrients are found along the coast of South America. The nutrients in these colder waters provide food for FISH, BIRDS, and other sea creatures living near the coast of South America. The cool waters also reduce the rate of EVAPORATION on the ocean surface and thus prevent much rain from falling on many coastal areas of northwestern South America.

During El Niño ocean winds called *trade winds* shift and push warmer Pacific Ocean waters toward the coast of South America. Several things happen when warmer water moves into this region. First, the warm waters do not provide as many nutrients as the cooler waters, and many ANIMALS starve. Second, the warm water provides more evaporation, causing heavy PRECIPITATION along the western coasts of North and South America. Finally, the loss of warm ocean waters along the coasts of Australia and southeast Asia results in severe drought conditions in those regions. [*See also* CLIMATE AND WEATHER.]

Endangered and Threatened Species ♣ A SPECIES whose POPULATION is so small that it may go extinct in the near future. An endangered species may be naturally rare or have small populations. Rare species are sensitive to changes in their ENVIRONMENT and slow to adapt to new conditions. Other endangered species require large areas of undisturbed land to survive and prosper, and are placed at risk by HABITAT LOSS. The introduction of exotic species and overhunting by humans also cause species to become endangered. A species is defined as threatened if its future survival is uncertain. [*See also* ENVIRONMENTAL LAWS; INVASIVE SPECIES; WILDLIFE REFUGES; WILDLIFE TRADE.]

Endemic Species ⚘ A SPECIES

native to a particular region or ENVI-RONMENT. Endemic species are unique to a specific region and often have small POPULATIONS that are very dependent on specific HABITATS and environmental conditions. Endemic species are sensitive to HABITAT LOSS and the introduction of exotic species, and are often at greater risk of extinction than other species. Some well-known endemic species include the tortoises of the Galápagos Islands and China's giant pandas. [*See also* ENDANGERED AND THREATENED SPECIES; INVASIVE SPECIES; KEYSTONE SPECIES.]

Energy Sources ⚘ Sources of energy that humans use to heat and cool their homes, run their cars and trucks, and power their factories and

Case Study: Wind Energy in California

Wind energy is becoming an increasingly popular ENERGY SOURCE, especially in California, which produces about 30 percent of the world's wind-generated electricity. WIND is turned into electricity with turbines, or special windmill-like structures with blades. Wind blowing against the blades causes them to spin, and this produces electricity. Turbines are usually grouped together in wind farms, which are located in the windiest parts of California. Wind energy does not cause air, land, or water pollution. Unlike fossil fuels, which will eventually run out, wind energy is renewable. The American Wind Energy Association estimates that wind farms built throughout the midwestern states would be able to produce electricity for the entire country.

Much of the energy in the western United States is generated by large dams, such as Grand Coulee Dam in Washington State.

farm equipment. Among the most common energy sources are non-renewable supplies of fossil fuels, such as petroleum, coal, and natural gas. Burning fossil fuels adds AIR POLLUTION in the form of carbon dioxide to the ATMOSPHERE and worsens the GREENHOUSE EFFECT. These energy sources are limited and will eventually run out.

There are several alternative sources of energy that do not have a harmful effect on the enviroment. These include solar energy, which comes from sunlight; geothermal energy, which comes from hot underground water; and wind-generated power.

Environment ☙
The external conditions that affect the growth, development, and survival of an ORGANISM or a POPULATION. The environment includes physical factors such as temperature, light, water, and nutrients.

Environmental Disasters ☙
Events that severely damage an ENVIRONMENT. Such disasters can devastate entire ECOSYSTEMS, causing harm to the area's land, water, and wildlife. Large environmental disasters can cause long-term, or even permanent, damage to the environment. Oil spills, for example, can kill many seabirds, otters, and other ANI-

After an oil spill, volunteers must work quickly to rescue birds and other animals.

MALS. Other wildlife can suffer serious long-term damage and may become endangered as the result of spills. ENVIRONMENTAL LAWS and ENVIRONMENTAL EDUCATION programs have been developed in almost every part of the world as a way to protect against environmental disasters.

Environmental Education ☙
Programs designed to bring the public in contact with nature and inform them about important environmental

issues such as ENDANGERED SPECIES, CONSERVATION, RECYCLING, and SUSTAINABLE DEVELOPMENT. Environmental education programs are organized and run by local nature centers, NATIONAL PARKS, WILDLIFE REFUGES, ECOTOURISM companies, and CONSERVATION ORGANIZATIONS.

Environmental Laws ⚘ Laws

that have been created to protect the natural ENVIRONMENT, including ENDANGERED SPECIES, certain HABITATS, and even whole ECOSYSTEMS. In the United States, laws controlling AIR POLLUTION and WATER POLLUTION have helped clean up and preserve the ATMOSPHERE and the nation's waterways. International laws have also made it illegal to collect or sell the ivory from ELEPHANT tusks or to kill many types of WHALES. [*See also* ENVIRONMENTAL EDUCATION.]

Epiphyte ⚘ A PLANT that grows on

or is attached to another plant. An epiphyte's ROOTS are found on the surface of their host plant rather than in the SOIL. Epiphytes absorb water and nutrients from the air and from rainwater running down the trunks of their host plants. Most epiphytes grow in moist, TROPICAL areas. Two familiar epiphytes are the Spanish moss that grows on oaks in subtropical regions and some of the orchids that grow in TROPICAL FORESTS.

Equator ⚘ An imaginary circle

around EARTH, an equal distance from the North and South Poles. The TROPICS include areas around the equator, north and south to the TEMPERATE zones. TROPICAL FORESTS and TROPICAL GRASSLANDS are found near the equator. Tropical HABITATS also experience fairly consistent warm and moist conditions throughout the year, although some locations have distinct dry and rainy SEASONS. [*See also* LATITUDE AND LONGITUDE.]

Erosion ⚘ The process by which SOIL

and ROCK are picked up and carried away by water, WIND, and ICE. Erosion generally occurs when the ground is bare and dry. It may be slow or very rapid, as when a sudden flood carves out a gully on a hillside.

Some COASTLINES and coastal areas are constantly damaged by erosion. Erosion also occurs in the DESERT, where water is scarce. Desert winds blow sand particles around, forming sand DUNES.

Vegetation helps prevent soil erosion. PLANTS cover and protect the ground from wind and rain, decreasing the amount of RUNOFF in an area. Plant ROOTS, especially those of GRASSES, also anchor the soil, keeping

Erosion threatens many coastal areas around the world. In some places, large portions of beach are lost to erosion each year.

it in place even against strong rains and winds. Human activities such as clearing TREES AND SHRUBS and irrigating of crops can greatly increase erosion and lead to loss of rich layers of soil. In extreme cases, human activities that lead to erosion can result in DESERTIFICATION, or the conversion of a formerly lush GRASSLAND into a desert.

Estuary
The place where a freshwater stream or river empties into an OCEAN, allowing fresh water and salt water to mix. Estuaries are often surrounded by MUD FLATS and salt MARSHES. Nutrients deposited by the river and during tidal movements make estuaries important HABITATS for many types of FISH, BIRDS, oysters, and crabs. Estuaries are also nurseries for many ocean fish and soft-shelled clams.

Eutrophication
A process in which a lake or pond gradually becomes shallower and filled with more PLANTS. Eutrophication occurs because lakes and ponds naturally tend to fill with silt deposits, which cause the water to becomes cloudier and more shallow. Eutrophication is speeded up when sediments, nitrogen, and phosphorus flow into a lake from surrounding farms. Certain plants, especially ALGAE, begin to grow profusely under these conditions and their bodies fill the water. Eutrophication can lead to the formation of a SWAMP or MARSH. This natural process can take thousands of years. [*See also* WETLANDS.]

Evaporation
Process that occurs when the temperature of a liquid, usually water, rises above a certain point, causing it to change into a

vapor, or gas. The rate of evaporation is affected by heat, humidity, and how much of the liquid is exposed to the air. Evaporation of water from OCEANS and FRESHWATER BIOMES is an important part of the WATER CYCLE.

Everglades 🌿 A WETLAND that once covered millions of acres of southern Florida. The Everglades are made up of many waterways, and they are dotted with ISLANDS covered with sawgrass and TREES. Near the Atlantic Ocean there are MANGROVE forests. Great expanses of watery grassland earned the Everglades the name "River of Grass." This huge wetland is home to many PLANTS and ANIMALS.

About 100 years ago, people began to drain and replace wetlands with a canal system. About one-half of the Everglades was converted to dairy and sugarcane farms, which increased WATER POLLUTION. Unnatural flooding from the canals and the rise in pollutants have caused cattails to replace much of the native sawgrass. In addition, the manatee, alligator, and Florida panther, which all live in the Everglades, have become endangered or threatened. One-fifth of the original Everglades has been set aside as the Everglades National Park.

Evolution and Extinction 🌿

Terms that refer to changes in natu-

Known as the "River of Grass," the watery Everglades is home to a great variety of plants and animals.

Case Study: The Galápagos Islands

Observation of the finches of the Galápagos Islands helped inspire the famous English scientist Charles Darwin to form his theories of evolution and NATURAL SELECTION. Darwin was intrigued by the fact that the islands had their own set of 14 BIRD species. The birds were all seed-eating finches, but each species had a special bill used to eat a different kind of food. Darwin thought the species had all evolved, or developed, from a common ancestor that had become stranded on one of the islands. He reasoned that the different inhabitants of the different islands, competition for food, and isolation from the original population led to the evolution of bills that could be used to eat different kinds of seeds. Over many generations these changes led to SPECIATION and the formation of 14 different finch species found nowhere else in the world.

ral POPULATIONS. Evolution is a change in the inherited traits in a population over the course of generations. Evolution can start with an accidental change, or mutation, that gives an ORGANISM a new trait that helps it stay alive and breed. Organisms without the new trait, or with a weaker form of it, are more likely to die or to produce unhealthy young. Over many generations the new trait spreads through the population and may even lead to SPECIATION, or the formation of one or more new SPECIES. Evolution results in populations that are able to thrive in particular HABITATS. The great diversity of BACTERIA, FUNGI, PLANTS, and ANIMALS on EARTH is the result of the evolution of many new species since life began millions of years ago.

Extinction is the death, or loss, of a species. Extinction is a natural process that can occur in response to crowding and competition for food, space, and shelter. It can also be caused by natural events such as volcanic eruptions, FIRES, droughts, and flooding. Mass extinctions, or the widespread loss of many similar species, occurred in the past due to harsh CLIMATE changes caused by events such as the ICE AGES. Human activities such as deforestation and POLLUTION, that destroy and disrupt natural ECOSYSTEMS, are now causing the extinction of many species. [*See also* ADAPTATION; NATURAL SELECTION.]

Exotic Species ⚘ *See* INVASIVE SPECIES.

Extinction ⚘ *See* EVOLUTION AND EXTINCTION.

Fauna ⚜ All of the ANIMALS found in a region. For example, a lake's fauna includes INSECTS, FROGS, many kinds of FISH, BIRDS, and certain MAMMALS. An area's fauna is closely related to its FLORA, or PLANT life. Animals are important to FOOD CHAINS AND WEBS in their roles as HERBIVORES, CARNIVORES, OMNIVORES, and SCAVENGERS.

Ferns ⚜ Seedless PLANTS that reproduce by forming spores, or small cells that develop into new individuals without fertilization. Fern leaves, called *fronds*, are divided into many parts. The fronds grow by uncurling their coiled tips, which are known as *fiddleheads*. There are more than 12,000 fern SPECIES in the world. Most grow in the TROPICS, but many are also found in TEMPERATE BROAD-LEAF FORESTS.

Fire ⚜ The light, heat, and flame produced by burning. Fires in FORESTS and GRASSLANDS occur naturally as the result of lightning or extreme heat. Humans also set fires on purpose to clear areas for AGRICULTURE or other use. Fires often occur in the summer, when temperatures are high, grounds are dry, and vegetation easily goes up in flames.

Forest managers used to view fires as bad and worked hard to prevent them. However, fire prevention programs disrupted natural growth, or SUCCESSION patterns, especially in

Wildfires burn thousands of acres of forest in the United States alone each year.

GRASSLANDS and some pine and RED-WOOD forests. Fire prevention can also lead to a buildup of dead, dry plant material that causes even more destruction if a fire starts. Scientists now recognize that fire is a natural event to which ORGANISMS adapt in most ECOSYSTEMS. For example, the seeds of some PLANTS, such as jack-pine trees and lodgepole pines, will not grow until after they have been exposed to the heat of fire.

Case Study: Fires in Yellowstone Park

On June 23, 1988, a lightening bolt ignited a fire in the southern area of Yellowstone National Park in Wyoming. Soon after, fire spread rapidly throughout the park, and over the next three months fires burned more than one million park acres.

The large fires of 1988 were not the first blazes in the park. The Yellowstone area has a steady fire history recorded as early as 1765. Most fires have been started by natural causes, such as lightning. Fire is necessary for the health and growth of the park's FLORA.

In the years after the fires, Yellowstone's ECOSYSTEM quickly reached a healthy state. New and different vegetation grew in the burned and cleared areas, providing new homes for the forest ANIMALS.

Fish

VERTEBRATES found in OCEANS, FRESHWATER BIOMES, and WETLANDS. Fish are an important food for aquatic PREDATORS and for humans. Some fish POPULATIONS have been seriously harmed by POLLUTION and overfishing.

Where Are They Found? Fish in the Desert

Australia's DESERT regions support approximately 33 native fish SPECIES. Many of these are found only in isolated populations. The eeltailed catfish, for example, is only found in 14 small springs around Dalhousie Springs, Australia.

Australian desert fish have many ADAPTATIONS that help them cope with the harsh, dry desert ENVIRONMENT. For example, most species spawn, or lay eggs, during the seasonal floods. These fish also migrate long distances to find suitable HABITATS when their water holes or streams dry out.

Most freshwater fish have very low tolerance for salt in their water, but high EVAPORATION rates in the desert can result in salty pools. Australia's desert fish have evolved the unusual ability to tolerate saltwater concentrations higher than that of the ocean. Australian desert fish also have a remarkable tolerance for high water temperatures. All can survive at temperatures of 95°F (35°C), and some even at 98°F (36.7°C).

The salmon of the Pacific Northwest perform an amazing migration upstream to spawn each year.

ton made of flexible cartilage, and *bony fish*. Most bony fish have bodies covered with scales. Bony fish are the dominant form of modern fish. There are about 20,000 SPECIES found in many diverse habitats worldwide. Some bony fish are predators, others filter nutrients from water, and some graze on PLANTS such as ALGAE. One bony fish, the remora, is a parasite that attaches to sharks. [*See also* MARINE ENVIRONMENTS.]

Floods and Flooding ❧ *See* WETLANDS.

Flora ❧ All of the PLANTS found in a region or geological period. An area's flora includes the ALGAE, MOSSES, LICHENS, FERNS, flowering plants such as GRASSES, wildflowers, weedy plants, bushes, and coniferous and broad-leaved TREES AND SHRUBS found in the region. The flora determines many of the environmental conditions, such as light and food supplies, that influence the FAUNA, or animal life, that can live in an area.

Fish are divided into three main groups. *Jawless fish*, such as lamprey and hagfish, have no jaws, no scales, and no paired fins. Hagfish are SCAVENGERS found in marine HABITATS. Lamprey are PARASITES that attach themselves to other fish. Lamprey have invaded the Great Lakes, where they have caused harm to native fish species.

The other two groups of fish are *cartilagenous fish*, which have skele-

Food Chains and Webs ❧ Terms that describe the path food takes through the ORGANISMS in an ECOSYSTEM. A food chain is a simple path, from one kind of PLANT through several kinds of ANIMALS. A food web is made up of many food chains.

Case Study: Changes in the Great Lakes Food Web

The Great Lakes form a large, interconnected inland waterway. Water flows east from Lake Superior into Lakes Huron, Erie, and Ontario. Water in Lake Ontario flows into the St. Lawrence River and out into the Atlantic Ocean. INVASIVE SPECIES introduced into one lake can quickly spread to the others, causing widespread disruption to lake food webs. In the past 200 years, more than 115 exotic species of PLANTS, FISH, ALGAE, and MOLLUSKS have entered the Great Lakes, mostly on shipping boats. Zebra mussels, for example, were released into Lake Huron in 1986. The mussels rapidly spread to the other Great Lakes and to parts of the Mississippi River. Zebra mussel populations grow rapidly, forming large colonies attached to hard surfaces. Lake food webs depend on tiny green PRODUCERS called PLANKTON, which zebra mussels filter out of the water for food. Scientists fear that large populations of zebra mussels will completely destroy the Great Lakes' producers, leaving little or no food for lake HERBIVORES such as snails, INSECTS, and many FISH. Without herbivores, lake CARNIVORES, from small dragonflies to much larger fish like salmon and trout, may also be left without enough food.

Food chain organisms are classified by TROPHIC LEVELS, or how they get food. Nutrients move from a PRODUCER, usually a green plant, to a primary CONSUMER, or plant-eating HERBIVORE, to a secondary consumer, or CARNIVORE. A pond food chain might involve a green ALGAE eaten by a snail that is then eaten by a BIRD. Organisms such as BACTERIA and FUNGI use the dead bodies and wastes from plants and animals as a source of food and return nutrients to the ENVIRONMENT. This is called DECOMPOSITION.

In nature the flow of foods usually follows a more complex pathway called a *food web.* An herbivore, for example, often eats several kinds of plants. Carnivores, such as FROGS, eat many different types of INSECTS and may, in turn, be food for a number of larger carnivores. When an ecosystem is damaged, important parts of its food webs are often destroyed, leaving its organisms without food.

Forest ⚘ A large area covered by TREES AND SHRUBS. BOREAL FORESTS have coniferous trees that can survive extremely cold winter weather. TEMPERATE BROADLEAF FORESTS are dominated by beech, maple, oak, or hickory trees. TROPICAL FORESTS are dominated by tall, fast-growing trees with shallow ROOTS.

(continues on p. 48)

Freshwater Biomes ❧ HABITATS

filled with water having low salt content, including lakes, rivers, streams, and ponds. Only 2 percent of the EARTH'S surface is covered with freshwater. Freshwater ECOSYSTEMS are home to many aquatic ORGANISMS. They also play an important role in the WATER CYCLE and are susceptible to many forms of POLLUTION. Humans use rivers, streams, lakes, and ponds for recreation, DRINKING WATER, and irrigation.

Rivers and Streams. Rivers and streams contain water that flows

Ducks are an essential part of freshwater biomes around the United States. The beautiful wood duck has recovered from the brink of extinction caused by habitat loss.

from a source to a place where it empties into either a large lake or an OCEAN. Source water is generally cold, clear, low in nutrients, and swift-flowing. ALGAE and trout are often found near the sources of rivers and streams. Downstream waters are wider, slower moving, warmer, and muddier, as well as home to more rooted PLANTS and FISH species.

Lakes and Ponds. The water in lakes and ponds is called *standing water* because it does not flow. Lakes and ponds form in basins, or depressions in the land where water collects. Lakes are deeper than ponds and cover more area. Their water can be divided into various zones based on light and depth.

Regions and Climate. Lakes, streams, rivers, and ponds are found around the world in widely scattered locations. The distribution of freshwater biomes is loosely related to annual PRECIPITATION. The greatest concentration of them is in rainforests. They are also common in the moister TEMPERATE regions, but are rarer in cold TUNDRA and POLAR REGIONS. Freshwater biomes are least abundant in DESERTS, although deserts may have oases or rivers flowing through them.

Plants. The plants found in freshwater habitats are those able to receive sufficient light for PHOTOSYNTHESIS. Tiny green plants called *phytoplankton* float near the water's surface, and ALGAE are the dominant PRODUCERS. MOSSES and flowering plants such as water lilies are also common. SEDGES and cattails are found around the edges of ponds.

Animals. Fish and aquatic INVERTEBRATES, such as snails and WORMS, are common in freshwater biomes. The larvae of many invertebrates go through their early stages of growth in lakes, ponds, rivers, and streams. FROGS, turtles, and water SNAKES are also abundant. Wading BIRDS, ducks, and geese often use freshwater habitats for feeding and nesting. MAMMALS such as otters, raccoons, BEAVERS, and hippos also inhabit freshwater biomes.

Human Impact. WATER POLLUTION and EROSION threaten the purity of many freshwater biomes. Humans also interfere with natural water flow by building dams, changing downstream ecosystems in the process. [*See also* WETLANDS; MARINE BIOMES; WATER POLLUTION; WATER CYCLE.]

Key Species: Dragonfly

Dragonflies are flying INSECTS with long, narrow, shiny wings and long, thin bodies found in meadows and ponds. They are CARNIVORES, eating insects that they catch with their legs while in flight. Dragonflies can fly up to 25 miles (40 kilometers) per hour. Males defend territories from other males. These territories are used to attract mates. Females lay their eggs in ponds by dipping their tails in the water. Young grow in the water, passing through several stages, and eating anything they can catch.

Biome Snapshot: Freshwater Biomes

Geographical Region: Found in in widely scattered locations around the world; distribution related to annual precipitation; the greatest concentration of streams, rivers, lakes, and ponds is found in rainforests and in the moister temperate regions; rivers, streams, lakes, and ponds are rarer in tundra, polar, and desert regions. **Climate, Precipitation, and Seasons:** Temperature and rainfall vary with geographical location; seasonal changes also reflect local conditions. **Dominant Plant Life:** Phytoplankton and algae are the major producers; mosses and flowering plants such as pond weeds, water lilies, and duck weed are also present; sedges and cattails are found around the edges of ponds. **Dominant Animal Life:** Fish and aquatic invertebrates, such as snails and worms; frogs, salamanders, and turtles are abundant; wading birds, ducks, and geese; river otters, raccoons, and beavers.

Forests determine many aspects of local and regional environmental conditions. For example, trees with deep roots help prevent EROSION. Trees also provide shelter for forest ANIMALS.

Fossil Fuels ⚜ *See* ENERGY SOURCES.

Freshwater Biomes ⚜ *See* PAGE 46.

Frogs ⚜ AMPHIBIANS that live both on land and in the water. Frogs are found in many HABITATS worldwide, especially in FRESHWATER BIOMES in TROPICAL and TEMPERATE regions. Tropical SPECIES may have skin in bright colors, and some tropical frogs secrete poisons through their skin. Frogs are ectotherms, or COLD-BLOODED animals, that are unable to survive the cold, harsh conditions of POLAR REGIONS and the TUNDRA.

Fungi ⚜ ORGANISMS that absorb nutrients through the body surface rather than by eating. Most fungi reproduce by forming small cells called *spores*. More than 50,000 SPECIES of fungi have been identified, but scientists think there may be as many as 250,000 species. Fungi range in size from single-celled yeasts to molds and rusts and the much larger mush-

Fungi play an important role in the ecosystem, decomposing organisms and recycling nutrients in the soil.

rooms. Most fungi are found on land, or in terrestrial HABITATS, but some are also found in watery areas.

Some fungi are decomposers, organisms that break down and then absorb nutrients from decaying matter. These fungi play an important role in recycling nutrients within an ECOSYSTEM. Other fungi are PARASITES, living in or on living organisms. Parasitic fungi attack and harm crop PLANTS, especially fruits, and cause human diseases such as athlete's foot. A third type of fungi are mutualists, which

Where Are They Found? Temperate Forests

Fungi flourish in the moist, damp HABI-TATS found in TEMPERATE BROADLEAF FORESTS. Larger fungi, such as shelf fungi, mushrooms, and puffballs, are found on the damp, shaded surfaces of tree trunks and growing in the soggy leaf litter on the forest floor. Other forest fungi invade moist dead trees, where they play important roles in the breakdown of wood, especially bark. Forest fungi also live in the SOIL, where they break down dead ORGANISMS, fallen leaves, and body wastes. These decomposers are important in releasing nutrients into the soil that can be absorbed and reused by PLANTS, especially FOREST trees. Another group of soil fungi lives inside the ROOTS of almost all plants, where they help change chemicals, such as nitrogen, into forms that can be used by their host plants.

means that they form beneficial partnerships with another SPECIES. The fungi found in LICHENS have formed such a relationship with ALGAE.

Genetic Engineering ⚘ Method

of moving genes, or genetic materials, from one SPECIES to a second species. Many scientists use genetic engineering to study diseases and to find new drugs to treat illnesses. Other scientists use genetic engineering to develop new crops and boost food supplies. Genetic engineering can be very beneficial to humans. However, some people are concerned that genetically engineered products may be harmful or that they may upset natural balances and cause damage to the environment.

Geography ⚘ The study of the surface of the EARTH, the location and distribution of living and nonliving things, and how they affect each other. The two major types of geography are physical geography and human geography. Physical geography studies the Earth's surface, land, and water. Human geography focuses on humans, the places they live, their customs, and how they use NATURAL RESOURCES.

Geology ⚘ The study of the structure of the EARTH and its origins and history. Geologists study the chemical composition of the Earth and examine how MOUNTAINS and OCEAN basins were formed. They also study how floods, GLACIERS, EARTHQUAKES, and VOLCANOES shape the Earth's surface. [*See also* GEOGRAPHY.]

Geysers and Hot Springs ⚘

Underground water that comes to

It may be the land of ice, but Iceland is most famous for its geothermal activity, which produces many hot springs and geysers. In fact, the word *geyser* comes from the name of Iceland's biggest geyser, the Great Geysir. Iceland has about 800 hot springs, more than any other country in the world. Some of Iceland's hot springs are geysers. The average temperature of the water that shoots out from most of Iceland's geysers is about 167°F (75°C).

One of the most famous geysers in the world is Old Faithful in Yellowstone National Park.

the EARTH's surface. Geysers shoot superhot water and steam in the air at random times. They are most common in areas with active VOLCANOES, such as Iceland, New Zealand, and the United States. Geysers form when GROUNDWATER comes in contact with the hot ROCKS under the earth's surface, or crust. The hot water turns into a powerful force that gushes through openings, or fissures, in the earth. A hot spring forms in an area where the groundwater seeps more gradually to the earth's surface after coming in contact with hot underground rocks. Geysers and hot springs are potential sources of geothermal energy. [*See also* ENERGY SOURCES.]

Glaciers ☙ Large bodies of ICE that slowly move over a wide area of land. Glaciers are usually found in the colder regions of the EARTH and on high MOUNTAIN ranges.

A glacier is a mass of ice that has been repeatedly covered and squeezed down by layers of snow. The melting of snow and ice during milder SEASONS causes the glacier to shrink. When the weather turns colder, the water refreezes. Repeated melting, refreezing, and new snowfalls cause the glacier to get bigger.

There are several types of glaciers, ranging from small ice fields to huge ice sheets called *continental*

Many of the world's glaciers lie between mountains like rivers of ice.

glaciers, which are found mainly in Greenland and Antarctica. Small pieces of a continental glacier may break off to form icebergs.

Glaciers move slowly, carrying ROCKS and debris along with them. During the ICE AGES, continental glaciers moved down from both poles. These glaciers altered the shape of many land formations, drastically changed global weather patterns, and altered entire BIOMES.

Scientists are concerned that the GREENHOUSE EFFECT will melt the glaciers. The melting of glaciers in Greenland and Antarctica may cause the level of the world's OCEANS to rise, which could pose a threat to coastal regions around the world.

Global Warming ⚘ *See* CLIMATE CHANGE; GREENHOUSE EFFECT.

Grasses ⚘ Family of PLANTS with stems; small clusters of flowers; fruits in the form of grains; and long, narrow, bladelike leaves. Grasses have ROOTS that form thread-like mats below ground. These roots hold water and nutrients in the SOIL and help prevent EROSION. Grasses are an important food for HERBIVORES, but they can be damaged by OVERGRAZING. There are about 9,000 grass SPECIES. They are the dominant plants in GRASSLANDS, which are found in TEMPERATE and TROPICAL regions. [*See also* TEMPERATE GRASSLANDS; TROPICAL GRASSLANDS.]

Grasslands ⚘ A type of BIOME dominated by GRASSES. Grasslands are found in regions where low annual rainfall and periodic FIRES hold back the growth of TREES AND SHRUBS. TEMPERATE GRASSLANDS, such as the prairies of North America, are found in regions with cold winters and hot summers. TROPICAL GRASSLANDS, also called *savannas*, cover large areas of

the interior of CONTINENTS north and south of TROPICAL rainforests. Grasslands provide HABITATS for many HERBIVORES and PREDATORS.

Grazing ⚘ *See* OVERGRAZING.

Great Barrier Reef ⚘ The largest CORAL REEF in the world, located in the Coral Sea off the coast of Queensland, Australia. It is composed of about 2,900 reefs that are separated from the Australian mainland by wide, deep lagoons and various ISLANDS.

The Great Barrier Reef is one of the most diverse MARINE BIOMES on earth. The reef provides HABITATS for 500 SPECIES of ALGAE, or seaweed, 400 coral species, 4,000 MOLLUSK species, 1,500 FISH species, and 215 species of BIRDS. POLLUTION and human activities have destroyed many parts of the reef. Scientists are also concerned that global warming may damage it.

Greenhouse Effect ⚘ Warming of the EARTH caused by an increase in certain gases, especially carbon dioxide, in the ATMOSPHERE. Human activities, such as the burning of fossil fuels and deforestation, have significantly increased the amount of such gases, which are known as *greenhouse gases*. Human activities have also increased the amounts of a group of chemical compounds known as CHLOROFLUOROCARBONS (CFC) in the atmosphere. The overall result of increased greenhouse gases and CFCs in the atmosphere has been a small but steady increase in global temperature called *global warming*.

The greenhouse effect may lead to drastic changes in CLIMATE AND

The largest coral reef in the world, the Great Barrier Reef of Australia, is one of the most diverse environments on Earth.

WEATHER patterns, major changes in the earth's BIOMES, the loss of many plant and animal SPECIES, and difficulty raising the farm crops humans depend on for food. Global warming has already caused melting of polar ICE and GLACIERS, which in turn may eventually cause a rise in sea levels that can damage COASTLINES.

Greenpeace ⚘ *See* CONSERVATION ORGANIZATIONS.

Groundwater ⚘ Water below the surface of the EARTH. Water from rain and snow either forms RUNOFF, which flows into rivers and streams, or soaks into the SOIL to form groundwater. An area's groundwater is held in an aquifer, a natural underground water storage area. Groundwater can be brought to the surface by digging wells, or it can rise to the surface in natural springs. Groundwater supplies can be tainted by POLLUTION from PESTICIDES, sewage, and other HAZARDOUS WASTES. [*See also* WATER CYCLE; WATER POLLUTION; WATER TABLE.]

Gymnosperms ⚘ *See* PLANTS.

Habitat

Habitat ⚘ The place where an ORGANISM lives. Habitat also refers to the ENVIRONMENT experienced by an organism, including such factors as CLIMATE AND WEATHER, temperature, OXYGEN, water, and SOIL. The quality of an organism's habitat is influenced by how many individuals of the same SPECIES live there, how much food there is to eat, and if the area is overcrowded. Each organism has ADAPTATIONS that permit it to tolerate, or withstand, normal habitat conditions. [*See also* HABITAT LOSS.]

Habitat Loss

Habitat Loss ⚘ The loss or destruction of a HABITAT due to human or natural activities. Habitat loss affects all ORGANISMS living in a particular habitat, as well as those in neighboring areas. Activities that cause habitat loss include deforestation, hunting, farming, LOGGING, overpopulation, OVERGRAZING, and FIRES. Almost every BIOME has been affected by habitat loss, which can cause the decline or even the extinc-

Case Study: Madagascar

MADAGASCAR, a large ISLAND nation, is found off the southeastern coast of Africa. It is home to about 5 percent of the Earth's total PLANT and ANIMAL species. Madagascar has suffered alarming HABITAT LOSS, mainly as the result of large increases in the human POPULATION there. The rainforests, in particular, have declined over the past 100 years from deforestation, LOGGING, hunting, and FIRES.

Over the past 1,000 years, 24 of Madagascar's ENDEMIC SPECIES have gone extinct. The lemurs, a group of animals closely related to monkeys, are found only on Madagascar. Fourteen lemur species are now extinct.

People have become increasingly aware of habitat loss as a serious national, even international, problem for Madagascar. Farmers, loggers, and local government have begun working with research teams to develop forest CONSERVATION plans that will help to protect the remaining habitats.

tion of many species. [*See also* EVOLUTION AND EXTINCTION.]

Hazardous Waste ⚘

Pollutants, sometimes also called toxic waste, that can damage the ENVIRONMENT or human health. Hazardous wastes can be liquid, solid, or gaseous. The cleanup or removal of toxic waste is often difficult and expensive. The United States has passed a number of laws aimed at regulating chemicals and other materials that contribute to hazardous waste. The best hope for dealing with the problem is for humans to adopt methods designed to decrease the amount of hazardous wastes produced and released into

Humans have not yet discovered a safe way to dispose of radioactive waste. Unless something is done, these wastes will pose a serious danger to the environment and to humans for centuries to come.

the environment. [*See also* AIR POLLUTION; POLLUTION; WATER POLLUTION.]

Herbivores ⚘

ANIMALS that only eat PLANTS, including GRASSES, the leaves and bark of TREES AND SHRUBS, ROOTS, fruits, and seeds. Herbivores include many INSECTS, seed-eating BIRDS, and certain MAMMALS such as deer. Herbivores often form the dominant animal groups in an ECOSYSTEM. They are primary CONSUMERS in FOOD CHAINS AND WEBS, and most of them serve as prey, or food, for CARNIVORES. Herbivores also contribute to ecosystems by acting as pollinators and by carrying plant seeds to new locations. [*See also* OMNIVORES.]

Hydrosphere ⚘

The water found on the surface of the EARTH and the moisture in the ATMOSPHERE. Earth's hydrosphere plays a vital role in supporting life. It includes the water in FRESHWATER BIOMES such as rivers, streams, ponds, and lakes; in WETLANDS such as MARSHES, SWAMPS, and BOGS; and in the saltwater that fills the OCEANS. The hydrosphere also includes the ICE, snow, and GLACIERS found in the POLAR REGIONS, on top of MOUNTAINS, and in the PERMAFROST on the frozen TUNDRA. [*See also* WATER CYCLE.]

Ice ✿ The solid form of water. Ice formed in the ATMOSPHERE falls to earth as snow, freezing rain, sleet, and hail. Ice and frost are major environmental factors that can harm and even kill many PLANTS, crops, fruits, and ANIMALS. All ORGANISMS need water to survive, and when water forms ice, it becomes unavailable for their use. The TUNDRA, with its permanent layer of ice, or PERMAFROST, and the icy POLAR REGIONS have fewer plant and animal SPECIES than other parts of the world.

Ice Ages ✿ Periods when the CLIMATE of the EARTH was much cooler and huge GLACIERS covered much of the land. There were four glacial periods, or ice ages, in Earth's history. The most recent ice age was during a period called the Pleistocene epoch, about 1.6 million years ago. At the height of the Pleistocene, about 30 percent of all land on Earth was covered by ice. The climate began to warm about 13,000 to 12,000 years ago, and by about 10,000 to 6,000 years ago most of the ice covering North America, Europe, and Asia had retreated—melted back—into the Arctic region. The ice ages changed some of Earth's BIOMES and caused the extinction of many BIRDS and other ANIMALS.

This girl is one of the Samburu people, an indigenous culture of Kenya.

Indigenous People ✿ People who are native to a particular area. Indigenous people make up about 10 percent of the world's human population and live on about 25 percent of the land. Examples of indigenous people include the Inuit of the TUNDRA regions, the Aboriginal people of Australia, and the Yanomani people of Brazil and Venezula.

Insects ✿ Small INVERTEBRATES with external skeletons (exoskeletons), six legs, and bodies divided into sections, or segments. The largest order of ANIMALS on EARTH, insects inhabit all kinds of HABITATS. There are more than a million known SPECIES of insects, and some scientists think there may be as many as 10 million on earth.

Honeybees help fertilize plants by spreading pollen from one plant to another as they gather pollen and nectar to make honey.

Adapted to virtually every habitat, insects play important roles in the FOOD CHAINS of many ECOSYSTEMS. They provide food for many other animals and pollinate many PLANTS. [*See also* POLLINATION.]

Invasive Species ⚘ Undesired ANIMALS or PLANTS that are not native to an area. Invasive species are also called *exotic species* or *introduced species*. Animals and plants in any ECOSYSTEM develop relationships among each other that result in a balance between PREDATORS and prey. Invasive species can disrupt this pattern and upset the natural balance of an ecosystem. Invasive species may eat plants or animals that the NATIVE SPECIES in an ecosystem depend on. They may introduce diseases that did not exist in that ecosystem before. They may also increase in number and crowd out native species.

Ecosystems are always changing, and new animals and plants come and go. But humans often increase the rate of change by introducing new invasive species, either by accident or on purpose. Ecosystems often cannot adjust to rapid change. This can re-

Case Study: Brown Tree Snake in Guam

Invasive species can cause major problems in an ECOSYSTEM. The brown tree snake is a native of Australia, New Guinea, and surrounding ISLANDS. In the 1940s or 1950s, it was accidentally introduced to the island of Guam, where it had a devastating effect on Guam's NATIVE SPECIES, particularly BIRDS. Within 40 years the snake had wiped out nine out of eleven native forest birds from the island.

sult in the extinction of SPECIES and serious damage to the ecosystem. [*See also* ENDEMIC SPECIES; EVOLUTION AND EXTINCTION.]

Invertebrates ⚘ ANIMALS lacking backbones and internal skeletons. These include arthropods (which include INSECTS, CRUSTACEANS, arachnids, and MOLLUSKS). Invertebrates make up 95 percent of all animals on earth and can be found in virtually all BIOMES. Invertebrates play important roles wherever they are found, providing food for other animals, pollinating PLANTS, and feeding on other animals. [*See also* VERTEBRATES.]

Octopi are among the largest invertebrates. This one was photographed near Papua, New Guinea. Invertebrates include insects, worms, and other creatures without backbones.

Some islands sustain species of plant and animal life found nowhere else on earth.

Islands ⚘ Bodies of land smaller than CONTINENTS that are completely surrounded by water. Islands of all shapes and sizes can be found in OCEANS, lakes, and rivers. The largest islands in the world are Greenland, New Guinea, Borneo, and MADAGASCAR. Islands contain all of the EARTH'S BIOMES. Small islands have just a single biome, while larger ones may have several.

Islands form in a number of different ways. Some form as a result of volcanic activity. Others are made up of old CORAL reefs. Still others may be parts of land that were originally attached to larger landmasses but were separated over long periods of time.

The PLANTS and ANIMALS found on islands are often originally from neighboring land areas. After reaching the island, they may start changing, or evolving, in ways that make them different from the original POPULATION. [*See also* ENDEMIC SPECIES; EVOLUTION AND EXTINCTION; INVASIVE SPECIES.]

Jellyfish ⚘ A group of INVERTE-
BRATE aquatic ANIMALS with bodies made up of a jelly-like substance. Jellyfish appear transparent, are mostly bell-shaped, and usually have hanging tentacles with stinging cells on the ends. Most species of jellyfish are found only in the OCEAN CURRENTS, which they use to float from place to place. Jellyfish may eat almost anything they can grab, depending on their size, from tiny floating animals to larger FISH.

Keystone Species ⚘ An ANIMAL
or PLANT that plays an important role in its ECOSYSTEM. If a keystone species is lost, its ecosystem may change dramatically. Keystone species are important because of their influence on other SPECIES.

A good example of a keystone species is the ELEPHANT of the African TROPICAL FOREST. Elephants have a very large impact on this ecosystem. They tear down trees and create clearings and pathways. Plants that need more light can grow

Elephants are a keystone species in parts of Africa because of the impact they have on the environment.

in these places, and other animals can use the pathways to move from place to place more easily. Elephants dig water holes, which other animals use. They also spread seeds so that new plants can grow. Without elephants in the FOREST, the plants and animals that have grown to depend on them could not survive. Plants can be keystone species as well. The oak tree is a keystone species in the TEMPERATE BROADLEAF FORESTS of North America.

Lakes ⚘ *See* FRESHWATER BIOMES.

Land Bridge ⚘ A narrow strip of land connecting two larger land areas. Land bridges are often covered by water at certain times. When the water level is low due to changes in CLIMATE, such as what occurs in an ICE AGE, the land is visible above the water. At that time ANIMALS can use the land bridge to cross from one larger land area to another. Scientists think that land bridges are one way that animals have migrated from place to place over long periods of time. Scientists also believe that early humans migrated to the Americas over a land bridge that connected Alaska and Siberia.

Landscape ⚘ The appearance of the EARTH's surface. Landscapes have distinctive features, such as MOUNTAIN ranges, valleys, hills, lakes, and plains. These features have been formed over time by geological processes and EROSION. Rivers, GLACIERS, and WIND also leave their marks on the landscape by carving into ROCKS and MOUNTAINS. The features of the landscape, together with CLIMATE AND WEATHER, help determine the BIOME of a particular area and the kinds of HABITATS it contains. HUMANS often change the appearance of landscapes by building roads and houses, planting lawns and trees, and damming rivers. [*See also* PLATE TECTONICS; TOPOGRAPHY.]

Latitude and Longitude ⚘ A system of imaginary intersecting lines used to locate places on the surface of the EARTH. Latitude lines run around the Earth's surface like belts, parallel to the EQUATOR both north and south of it. Measured in degrees, latitude measurement tells how far north or south of the equator you are. Longitude lines are also called *meridians.* They run in a north-south direction around the Earth and intersect latitude lines. Longitude is also measured in degrees.

Any point on a map of the earth has both a longitude and latitude measurement. Latitude is usually more important than longitude in shaping the Earth's BIOMES. This is because latitude indicates distance from the equator and the north and south poles, which is more directly related to temperature and CLIMATE.

Legumes ⚘ Kinds of PLANTS with podlike fruit that typically splits easily in half. The pods of legumes are often used as food by both humans and ANIMALS. Legumes include such plants as peas, beans, and peanuts.

Most plants depend on nitrogen in the SOIL as an essential nutrient for growth. Legumes have evolved the ability to take nitrogen out of the air as well. They do this with the help of special BACTERIA living in their ROOTS. Because of this ability, legumes can grow in areas with less fertile soil, where other plants may not be able to grow. [*See also* MUTUALISM; NITROGEN CYCLE.]

Lichens ♨
Small plants made up of FUNGI and ALGAE growing together in a close relationship that benefits

Often found on rocks and trees, lichens are made up of fungi and algae growing together in a close relationship.

both. This kind of relationship is known as *symbiosis*. These ground-hugging plants often grow in patches on ROCKS, wood, and SOIL in TEMPERATE BROADLEAF FORESTS and TROPICAL FORESTS as well as in cold TUNDRA regions and on MOUNTAINS.

The two parts of a lichen work together. The algae creates food using PHOTOSYNTHESIS, while the fungus gathers nutrients from the surrounding environment. This relationship allows lichens to grow in places where many plants cannot grow. Lichens also play an important role in weathering, the breaking down of rocks and trees into soil. [*See also* MUTUALISM.]

Life Cycle ♨
The series of stages a PLANT, ANIMAL, or other ORGANISM goes through in the course of its lifetime. Some animals change only in size, becoming larger as they grow older. Other animals, such as butterflies and FROGS, change their forms completely from birth to death.

Life Zone ♨
An area, region, or HABITAT that shares certain physical or biological features, such as rainfall, temperature, and dominant vegetation. Life zones are smaller than BIOMES. They are called by such names as *lowland tropical wet forest* or *tropical mountain humid forest*.

People define and study life zones in order to better understand, manage, and conserve natural areas.

Lithosphere ♣ The outermost rocky layers of the Earth's surface. Earth is composed of a number of distinct layers. The innermost part of the Earth is the interior core, which scientists believe consists of dense molten iron. The lithosphere lies above the core. The topmost layer is the crust, an area of solid ROCK that forms the foundation for the CONTINENTS. Beneath the crust is a thick layer of rock known as the *mantle*. The lithosphere is where the process of PLATE TECTONICS occurs, which produces VOLCANOES and a gradual movement of the continents called *continental drift*. The uppermost portion of the lithosphere is also where all the Earth's BIOMES are found. [*See also* HYDROSPHERE.]

Logging ♣ The process of cutting down trees for timber. Logging is a major cause of FOREST destruction worldwide, and it greatly affects forest ECOSYSTEMS. When many or all of the trees are removed—a process called *deforestation*—many PLANTS and animal HABITATS are destroyed.

The world's forests are increasingly threatened by logging activities. This log train is in Washington State.

The logging roads used to get trucks and other equipment in and out of forests also divide and damage wildlife habitats.

Clearcutting is a method of logging where all the trees from an area are cut down at one time. There are less destructive methods of logging, however. *Sustainable logging* is a method of removing only selected trees, leaving some of the forest intact. Sustainable logging methods can minimize harmful impacts on ecosystems.

Longitude ♣ *See* LATITUDE AND LONGITUDE.

Madagascar ❧ The world's fourth largest ISLAND, Madagascar is home to a unique group of PLANTS and ANIMALS. Many of these have evolved in isolation from the rest of the world. Madagascar's BIOLOGICAL DIVERSITY is especially rich because of its many different HABITATS. The island contains TROPICAL FORESTS, woodlands, and dry FORESTS, as well as other ECOSYSTEMS.

Mammals ❧ WARM-BLOODED ANIMALS that give birth to live young and feed their babies milk from the mother's body. There are about 4,000 known SPECIES of mammals, from the smallest field mouse to the largest animal living on EARTH—the blue whale. Mammals live in all BIOMES on Earth. They have a wide variety of ADAPTATIONS and a broad range of sizes and behaviors. Many mammals are endangered due to POLLUTION and HABITAT LOSS caused by human activities.

Mangroves ❧ TROPICAL SPECIES of tree that live along OCEAN coasts and in saltwater MARSHES. They are

Tigers are meat-eating carnivores. These large mammals are threatened by destruction of their habitats, poaching, and other human activities.

adapted to harsh, salty environments where many other PLANTS cannot grow. Many mangrove trees have ROOTS that extend up from the trunk of the tree through the air instead of growing into the SOIL. They grow this way because they have adapted to soil with little OXYGEN and get oxygen directly from the air. Mangroves grow primarily in tropical and subtropical areas, where they provide HABITATS for many BIRDS, MAMMALS, and FISH.

Marine Biomes ⚘ Saltwater

OCEANS and seas cover about 70 percent of the EARTH'S surface. These large bodies of water have fairly stable temperatures compared to some land HABITATS.

Marine biomes are subdivided into three zones. The intertidal zone is a shallow area found at the edge of the sea, where waves wash over sand and ROCKS. ORGANISMS living in this zone, such as barnacles and green ALGAE, must be able to survive extremes of heat, moisture, and salinity. The benthic zone is the area at the bottom of the sea. Most marine PLANTS and ANIMALS live in the shallower portions of the benthic zone. The pelagic zone includes the open sea. Here are found animals such as squid, sea turtles,

The intertidal zones of marine environments provide fish and other food for many bird species.

tunas, and WHALES, as well as tiny organisms called PLANKTON that drift near the surface of the water.

Regions and Climate. There are four major OCEAN basins—the Atlantic, Pacific, Indian, and Arctic Oceans. The Mediterranean, Caribbean, Bering, Arabian, and South China Seas are smaller bodies of water found in the marine biome.

Ocean water temperature varies, from 28°F (–2°C) in cold regions to about 86°F (30°C) or higher in hot regions. Surface water temperatures are more changeable, while the temperature of the water beneath the surface stays fairly constant. These differences in temperature contribute to the creation of OCEAN CURRENTS, which play a role in determining patterns of air movement and water circulation over large portions of the Earth.

Plants. The number and kinds of marine plants found in a particular area are limited by the amount of light available in the water and the salt-tolerance of the plants. Sea grasses are one of the few flowering plants found in marine habitats. There are many seaweeds in intertidal zones. Tiny drifting plants called *phytoplankton* are found on vast stretches of the surface of the sea. These plants perform most of the

PHOTOSYNTHESIS that occurs in marine biomes.

Animals. The oceans are home to some interesting MAMMALS, including seals, walruses, dolphins, and whales. Many other kinds of animals also are found in the oceans and seas, including FISH, CRUSTACEANS, jellyfish, and corals. Penguins are found in the colder waters of the southern hemispheres. Zooplankton form the animal portion of the plankton found in marine biomes.

Human Impact. Earth's marine biomes are threatened by many human activities. When humans alter ocean shorelines to build houses, it often disturbs animal habitats. Over-fishing has destroyed many fish, dolphin, and whale POPULATIONS. PESTICIDES, human wastes, and other pollutants carried by rivers and streams into the oceans can cause chemical and physical changes that threaten the survival of marine life.

Key Species: Sharks

The shark is a kind of FISH found in oceans and in some FRESHWATER BIOMES. These animals are CARNIVORES. They use their powerful jaw muscles and sharp teeth to capture and eat prey. Sharks also have special organs called *electroreceptors* that help them find prey. These organs are sensitive to weak electrical fields created by the breathing and movements of the prey. Among the best-known SPECIES of shark are the tiger, hammerhead, mako, and great white shark.

Biome Snapshot: Oceans

Geographical Regions: Oceans and seas are found worldwide; the oceans and seas can be viewed as forming one large interconnected ocean system. **Climate:** Varies with area, from very cold polar regions to more moderate temperate oceans and seas to very warm tropical oceans. **Diversity:** Varies from very diverse tropical coral reefs and rocky intertidal regions to sparsely populated deep-sea regions. **Dominant Plants:** Limited to seagrasses, algae, and phytoplankton. **Dominant Animals:** Great diversity of animal species, including many animal groups not found in other biomes. Small, simple invertebrates, such as sponges and jellyfish; medium-size invertebrates, such as lobsters, sea stars, octopuses, and squid; many fish, including tunas, sharks, rays, and barracudas; marine birds, including penguins, albatrosses, gulls, and terns; and marine mammals such as whales and dolphins.

Marine Mammals ⚮ MAMMALS

that spend the majority of their lives in OCEANS and seas. Seals, sea lions, WHALES, dolphins, and manatees are all marine mammals. These animals are uniquely adapted to life in the ocean. They have streamlined bodies and strong flippers for swimming, thick layers of fat to protect them from the cold, and oily skins to make them slip easily through the water. Most marine mammals eat FISH. Many are highly endangered due to extensive hunting and WATER POLLUTION.

Marine Sanctuaries ⚮ Saltwater

ECOSYSTEMS protected by law. Like NATIONAL PARKS on land, marine sanctuaries are designed to preserve and protect unique ocean HABITATS and their PLANTS and ANIMALS from POLLUTION and other disturbances. Marine sanctuaries in the United States exist in areas from the Florida Keys to the Hawaiian Islands. They protect CORAL REEFS, sea lions, sea turtles, breeding and feeding grounds for millions of MARINE MAMMALS, and MIGRATION routes for WHALES and other animals.

Marsh ⚮ A warm coastal WETLAND

with dense aquatic PLANTS such as GRASSES and cattails. These plants must have ROOTS adapted to spending a large portion of their time underwater. Marsh plants make excellent food for vegetation-eating ANIMALS and attract a lot of wildlife. Many kinds of BIRDS, REPTILES, and AMPHIBIANS depend on marshes for shelter and food.

Marsupials ⚮ A unique group of

MAMMALS that carry their young in a pouch following birth. Marsupial babies are born much smaller and less developed than other mammals. They complete their development while inside the mother's pouch.

There are about 260 SPECIES of marsupials worldwide, found only in the Americas, Australia, and New

Most species of marsupials, including koala bears, are found in Australia and New Zealand.

Where are They Found? Marsupials in the Australian Grasslands

Australia supports a more diverse POPULATION of marsupials than any other place on EARTH. They inhabit virtually all of Australia's available HABITATS, including DESERTS, FORESTS, and GRASSLANDS. Grassland marsupials include about 50 SPECIES of kangaroos and wallabies, which are known for their short forelimbs, powerful hopping legs, and long, strong tails that help provide balance. Their strong legs allow them to bound through the GRASSES, moving easily and quickly, like pogo sticks. However, this ADAPTATION means that they are not very good at walking!

Kangaroos and wallabies are HERBIVORES, feeding primarily on grasses and leaves. They give birth to one young at a time. It is born quite small and undeveloped and grows while living in its mother's pouch for several more months.

Zealand. They include opossums, marsupial moles, koalas, bandicoots, and kangaroos. While marsupials eat mostly PLANTS and some INSECTS, a number of marsupials are CARNIVORES.

Microorganisms ⚘ Tiny PLANTS or ANIMALS that can be seen only with a microscope. Microorganisms include BACTERIA, some ALGAE, yeasts, and viruses. Many microorganisms are one-celled organisms, but they also can be multicelled. Microorganisms live everywhere on EARTH: in SOIL, water, air, food, and even inside other living things. Amazingly, the human body is home to more bacteria microorganisms than to human cells. Microorganisms perform many essential services in all BIOMES. This includes decomposing, or breaking down, dead organisms into nutrients in soil, and breaking down toxic wastes and chemicals in water.

Migration ⚘ A seasonal mass movement of ANIMALS from one area to another. Animals typically migrate in search of food or breeding grounds.

There are different kinds of migrations. Animals can move in one direction and never return to the place they began, or they can move randomly from place to place. Another kind of migration is when a group of animals seasonally travels between two particular places. For example, many BIRDS are known for their long migratory flights from one CONTINENT to another. Many other animals also migrate, including FISH such as salmon and eels, MARINE MAMMALS like seals and whales,

Case Study: Gray Whale Migration

The gray whale makes one of the most dramatic migrations known, traveling more than 12,000 miles (19,300 kilometers) between its northern feeding grounds in the Bering and Chukchi seas near Alaska and its southern breeding grounds off the coast of California. Traveling in small groups known as *pods* (3 to 16 whales), they spend the winter in the warm, TROPICAL seas, mating and giving birth to their calves. In summer they travel to feeding grounds in the cold arctic waters up north. This migration can take from 2 to 3 months. The gray whale is a bottom feeder, scraping the OCEAN floor to find small CRUSTACEANS and MOLLUSKS. For months while migrating, however, gray whales eat very little and live off their thick layer of blubber.

lusk SPECIES. Most mollusks are OMNIVORES and eat just about anything. Mollusks are found in MARINE BIOMES, FRESHWATER BIOMES, and on land in terrestrial HABITATS. They come in a great range of sizes, from tiny snails to giant squid.

Moon ⚘
The EARTH's only natural satellite. The Moon circles once around the Earth approximately every 28 days. Its surface is covered by craters, MOUNTAINS, ROCKS, and other material from collisions with asteroids (large space rocks) and other planetary debris.

The gravitational pull of the Moon causes the cycle of TIDES in the

and INSECTS such as the monarch butterfly.

Mollusks ⚘
A large group of INVERTEBRATE animals with soft, one-part bodies, gills to breathe, and a special foot that some use to move around. In squid and octopuses, this foot has evolved into long, arm-like tentacles. There are an estimated 50,000 mol-

Beautiful to look at in the night sky, the Moon affects the Earth in a number of ways. One of the most important is its role in producing tides in the Earth's oceans.

Earth's OCEANS and thus affects tidal ECOSYSTEMS. High tides occur in a particular place when the Moon is closest to that place.

Mosses ☘ Simple, small PLANTS that grow in tight, spongy mats close to the ground. Mosses prefer moist, shady places and BOGS. They attach to the ground or ROCKS by long threadlike structures called *rhizoids*. Mosses do not have ROOTS or water-bearing tissues. Instead, they absorb water directly into each part of their body. Most mosses are found in TROPICAL areas. However, they are also found in TEMPERATE regions, and a few live in POLAR REGIONS.

Mosses are a very diverse group of plants, with more than 10,000 SPECIES. One of the bettter known species is sphagnum moss. Also called peat moss, sphagnum moss forms part of the floating mats found in bogs. Peat moss absorbs 15 to 20 times its weight in water. It also creates a warm, acidic, low-OXYGEN environment that other bog ORGANISMS must be able to tolerate.

Mosses play an important role in their ECOSYSTEMS. They help reduce EROSION by holding SOIL in place. They cycle water and nutrients, and they also help to break down rocks into new soil. [*See also* WETLANDS.]

Mountain Biome ☘ *See* PAGE 70.

Mud Flats ☘ Flat or nearly level tidal zones usually found near ESTUARIES, quiet bays, and lagoons. Mud flats generally experience very little wave action. They are made of fine sand grains, silt, clay, and dead organic material. BACTERIA and FUNGI living in the mud use up OXYGEN supplies while breaking down organic matter. This creates anaerobic conditions just below the surface. The anaerobic part of a mud flat is black and smells like rotten eggs. ANIMALS found living in mud flats include soft-shelled clams, lugworms, and ghost shrimp. [*See also* WETLANDS.]

Mutualism ☘ A type of relationship between two SPECIES in which both benefit each other in terms of survival and reproduction. Mutualism is a form of symbiosis. For example, in Central America some ANTS live in the thorns of acacia trees and use the trees' nectar as food. The ants, in turn, bite and sting other HERBIVORES that land on the trees. Another example: Microbes that live inside TERMITES get nutrients from and are protected by their termite host. The host benefits because the microbes break down and release nutrients from the wood eaten by the termite. [*See also* LICHENS.]

Mountain Biome

Raised areas of land with high, steep sides. Most mountains are formed when enormous sections of the EARTH'S crust, called *tectonic plates*, push against one another. Some mountains are VOLCANOES formed when openings in the earth eject lava, ash, and large ROCKS.

Mountains cover about one-fourth of the Earth's surface. Some mountains stand alone, while others are grouped into ranges. Some are fairly young, others are very old.

Regions. There are mountains on every CONTINENT as well as on many OCEAN floors. The Himalaya Mountains of Asia contain some of the world's highest mountains. The Alps are one of the major mountain ranges of Europe. The Andes of South America are the longest mountain range on earth. North America has two major mountain ranges, the Rocky Mountains in the west and the Appalachian Mountains in the east.

Climate. Mountains have a great range of CLIMATE AND WEATHER conditions. PRECIPITATION and temperature vary with ALTITUDE, or elevation. Changing conditions cause differences in PLANT and ANIMAL life as one moves up a mountain. Plant and animal communities at different elevations resemble the BIOMES seen as one moves from the EQUATOR to the POLAR REGIONS. A single mountain may have conditions similar to DESERTS or TROPICAL FORESTS at the bottom, BOREAL FORESTS at higher elevations, and year-round snow or polar conditions at the top.

Plants. Mountain plant life depends on elevation and where in the

Majestic mountain ranges, such as the Grand Tetons in Wyoming, often have a great range of climate and weather conditions, which support diverse plant and animal life.

Key Species: *Mountain Goats*

Mountain goats live above the TREELINE in the Rocky Mountains, where they eat GRASSES and other PLANTS. These MAMMALS have white, wooly coats and black, curved horns. Mountain goats have hooves that are thin on the outside and filled with an inner, soft pad. With amazing balance, they run and jump easily in steep, rocky areas.

world a mountain is located. The TREES AND SHRUBS found at each elevation on a mountain depend on temperature, rainfall, and SOIL. WIND and exposure are also important. Higher elevations are dominated by alpine TUNDRA plants such as MOSSES and LICHENS. Rocky Mountain FORESTS have mostly coniferous trees such as spruce, firs, and pines. The Appalachian Mountains have mostly TEMPERATE BROADLEAF FORESTS.

Animals. Large HERBIVORES such as big horn sheep, mountain goats, deer, elks, yaks, and the ibex are common in mountain HABITATS. Smaller herbivores, such as pika, mice, voles, marmots, and flying squirrels are also common. Grizzly bears and black bears are the largest OMNIVORES found on mountains. Endangered PREDATORS such as snow leopards and wolves are much less common. Mountains with temperate broadleaf forests are often home to many kinds of BIRDS.

Human Impact. In the United States and Canada, millions of acres of mountain habitat are protected as NATIONAL PARKS and national forests. However, mountain wildlife and forests are still at risk from LOGGING, EROSION, and various human activities. The GREENHOUSE EFFECT and ACID RAIN also have harmful effects on mountain forests and lakes. [*See also* AIR POLLUTION; PLATE TECTONICS.]

Biome Snapshot: *Mountains*

Geographical Region: Worldwide, on all continents and on ocean floors. **Altitude:** Range in elevation up to 29,028 feet (8,848 meters) on Mount Everest. **Climate and Precipitation:** Temperature and rainfall change with elevation, from tropical or temperate conditions at lower elevations to tundra and polar conditions at mountain peaks. **Dominant Plant Life:** Varies with climate and location; often grassland species at the base, then broadleaf forests replaced by boreal forests and alpine tundra species. **Dominant Animal Life:** Large herbivores such as mountain goats, bighorn sheep, yaks, ibex, elk, deer; bears; a few predators; abundant life.

National Forests ❧ *See* PUBLIC LANDS.

National Parks ❧ Land and coastal areas with great scenic, environmental, or historical significance that are protected by law. In the United States, these parks are managed by the National Park Service. Notable national parks in the United States include Yellowstone National Park in Wyoming, Grand Canyon Na-

National parks such as the Grand Canyon are landmarks of great scenic beauty that also protect the habitats of many plants and animals.

tional Park in Arizona, Yosemite National Park in California, the Hawaii Volcanoes National Park, and Glacier National Park in Montana.

Many American national parks were first set aside for important geological and scenic attractions, not for their living ORGANISMS. Today the Park Service tries to protect a park's scenic areas and wildlife while also letting the public in for hiking, camping, and other outdoor activities. Some national parks are managed in ways that allow their HABITATS to undergo natural SUCCESSION and FIRES. In addition to national parks, the United States has set aside other places because of their natural or historic importance. These include national seashores, national monuments, national historic sites, national preserves, and national battlefields. [*See also* PUBLIC LANDS; WILDLIFE REFUGES.]

Native Species ❧ ORGANISMS naturally found in an area. Native species, also called *indigenous species*,

are well adapted to conditions in their ECOSYSTEMS. They play important roles in regional FOOD CHAINS AND WEBS and are very important to their communities. Certain native species may be characteristic of a particular ecosystem, such as the MANGROVE trees found in mangrove SWAMPS or cactus plants in a DESERT. Native species only found in small areas are at greater risk when their HABITATS are disturbed. [*See also* ENDEMIC SPECIES; INVASIVE SPECIES.]

Natural Resources ⚘ Materials

such as air, water, food, PLANTS, SOIL, and minerals that support life. Humans depend on living creatures in many ways—for food, the OXYGEN provided by plants, and natural activities such as the water cleansing provided by MARSH plants. Humans also use products derived from living organisms, such as lumber, medicines, and other substances, to support and improve their lives.

Some natural resources, such as the energy in sunlight, are renewable, which means that they are continuously replenished and not used up. Other resources, such as water and soil, and living ORGANISMS are renewable as long as humans use them wisely. Nonrenewable resources are found in only limited amounts on Earth. Examples include

To exploit natural resources, including the copper from this open-pit mine in Montana, humans often change the landscape.

fossil fuels such as coal and minerals such as metals and clay. Nonrenewable resources will be gone forever if humans overuse them. [*See also* POPULATION; POLLUTION; RECYCLING; PUBLIC LANDS; SUSTAINABLE DEVELOPMENT.]

Natural Selection ⚘ A major force

of evolution that can change the appearance or behavior of a group of ORGANISMS. In any POPULATION, some individuals have inherited traits that make it easier for them to stay alive and to breed. Two things happen to individuals without these traits, especially in harsh conditions: they may die, or they may produce fewer young. Over many generations, every SPECIES is shaped by the inherited ADAPTATIONS that make them most likely to succeed in their particular BIOME, HABITAT, or NICHE. [*See also* EVOLUTION AND EXTINCTION.]

Niche ♣ The parts of an ENVIRONMENT that are important for the survival of a SPECIES or POPULATION. The word *niche* also refers to the role an ORGANISM plays in an ECOSYSTEM, which consists of all the niches filled by the organisms living there.

Case Study: Spotted Owl

The threatened spotted owl lives in dense FORESTS in the northwest United States. It has a very specialized niche and cannot tolerate change. Each breeding pair needs 1,400 to 4,500 acres of forest to survive. The survival of the species is threatened because much of its HABITAT has been destroyed by the LOGGING industry and reduced by other human activities. In 1993 the government drastically cut back how much logging could occur on federal lands. The spotted owl's decline has slowed a lot since then. But the species is encountering a new threat in the form of competition from a larger owl species, the barred owl, which has expanded its range into the spotted owl's already limited habitat.

For a PLANT, a niche is not only the place where it is found but also how much light, water, and chemicals are available to it for its survival. For example, a cactus in the DESERT has ADAPTATIONS that allow it to tolerate intense heat and low water supplies. For most ANIMALS, a niche includes where it lives, what it eats, how hard it is to find food and mating partners, and the kinds of shelter it uses.

Organisms do not always occupy the same niche throughout their lifetimes. For example, a young komodo dragon is a small tree-dwelling lizard that feeds on INSECTS. An adult komodo dragon is a large ground-dwelling lizard that preys on large animals.

Species with very similar niches compete with one another for space, food, and other resources. Intense competition may lead one species to change, or evolve. The result is that it no longer has to struggle so hard to get the things it needs to survive.

Nitrogen Cycle ♣ A NUTRIENT CYCLE involving the movement of nitrogen through the ENVIRONMENT. Nitrogen is a critical nutrient that influences PLANT and ANIMAL life in every BIOME on EARTH. Nitrogen gas makes up about 80 percent of Earth's ATMOSPHERE.

All living ORGANISMS need nitrogen to make proteins, but most cannot use nitrogen in the form of a gas. Special BACTERIA live in the ROOTS of some PLANTS such as LEGUMES. These bacteria are called *nitrogen-fixing bacteria* because they change nitrogen gas into forms of nitrogen that plants can use to make proteins. Animals get the nitrogen they need from eating plants or other animals.

Decomposers in the soil break down the proteins in waste materials and the dead bodies of animals and change them back into forms of nitrogen. Some of this nitrogen may be taken up by plants. A special type of bacteria, called *denitrifying bacteria,* changes some of this waste material back into nitrogen gas, which returns to the atmosphere.

Humans interfere with the nitrogen cycle when they add large amounts of nitrogen fertilizers to their crops, lawns, and golf courses. Nitrogen RUNOFF from these areas can pollute GROUNDWATER, lakes, and streams. Water treatment plants also add large amounts of dissolved nitrogen to rivers and streams. [*See also* CONSUMERS; DECOMPOSITION; WATER POLLUTION.]

Nutrient Cycle ♣ The movement of chemicals vital for life from the ENVIRONMENT into living ORGANISMS

and back to the environment. For example, PLANTS use the carbon dioxide, water, and minerals found in the SOIL and ATMOSPHERE to produce sugars and starches. In the process they release OXYGEN into the atmosphere, and this is used by other organisms. When ANIMALS eat the plants, their bodies release undigested plant matter to the ground. Decomposers in the soil break this material down and release the chemicals back into the environment.

Human activities often interfere with nutrient cycles, making it difficult for organisms to get the chemicals they need to survive. Dams and irrigation divert water from the WATER CYCLE. Overuse of fertilizers high in nitrogen and phosphorus can disrupt normal nutrient cycles. Excessive use of fossil fuels releases too much carbon into the atmosphere. [*See also* CARBON CYCLE; DECOMPOSITION; NITROGEN CYCLE.]

Ocean Currents ♣ The flow of sea water in a particular direction or path. Currents stir and mix OCEAN waters, distributing food, nutrients, and OXYGEN needed by sea creatures. Ocean currents also affect global CLIMATE AND WEATHER patterns.

Surface water currents are moved by prevailing winds and the turning, or rotation, of the EARTH on its axis. One such current is the Gulf Stream, which moves warm water from the TROPICS north and then east into the North Atlantic Ocean. Larger, slower moving currents are found deeper in the oceans and run in the opposite direction to surface currents. These currents seem to replace water that has been moved away by surface currents. Currents of this sort move water along the EQUATOR. The regular movement of ocean waters along the seashore, known as *longshore currents*, renews beaches with fresh deposits of sand and other sediments.

Changes in ocean currents can have an important impact on global temperature and climate patterns. One example is EL NIÑO, which often causes flooding in dry areas and droughts in places that are usually wet. Ocean currents also play an important role in FOOD CHAINS AND WEBS, carrying FISH and nutrients such as PLANKTON around the oceans. The currents also carry pollutants, however, caused by human activities. [*See also* MARINE BIOMES.]

Oceans ☙ Vast bodies of salt water that cover about 75 percent of the EARTH. About 97 percent of all the water on Earth is in oceans. Oceans contain mountain ranges, enormous VOLCANOES, and abundant marine life. They are essential to the survival of humans and other forms of life on Earth.

Water enters oceans as part of the WATER CYCLE. When rain or other forms of PRECIPITATION fall on the ground, some of the water evaporates into the air, some soaks into the SOIL, and the rest forms RUNOFF that eventually empties into the oceans.

Oceans are MARINE BIOMES that provide HABITATS for many forms of sea life. Deep ocean areas are often home to large ANIMALS such as WHALES AND DOLPHINS. Other marine creatures are found on the bottom of shallower parts of the the ocean, near shore, and floating on the surface of the ocean. CORAL REEFS are found in shallow, clear, warm TROPICAL parts of the oceans. They often cover large areas and provide homes for many kinds of ALGAE, INVERTEBRATES, and FISH.

Old-growth Forests ☙ Also called mature forests. Old-growth forests are areas that have reached the end point of SUCCESSION. These FORESTS have shown few changes in plant or animal SPECIES over a long period of time. The term *old-growth forest* is also used to describe a forest that has either never been cut or lumbered, or has remained in a natural condition for many years.

Old-growth forests in the United States have huge trees that are hundreds or even thousands of years old.

Old-growth forests provide important HABITATS for many creatures. The most famous species linked to old-growth forests is the spotted owl, an endangered species that lives in dense old-growth forests in the Pacific Northwest. This species of owl has been the focus of a conflict between people who wish to cut old-growth forests for timber and people who wish to keep the forests and their ECOSYSTEMS intact. [*See also* ENDANGERED AND THREATENED SPECIES; NICHE; TREES AND SHRUBS.]

Omnivores ⚘ ANIMALS with a diet that includes both PLANTS and other animals. Unlike the more specialized members of FOOD CHAINS AND WEBS, omnivores have more choices of food. Rats, pigs, bears, certain BIRDS, and humans are all omnivores. Many omnivores have keen senses of smell and taste, which makes it easier for them to find a variety of foods.

Organism ⚘ Any living creature. An organism may be made of a single cell, as BACTERIA are. FUNGI, PLANTS, and ANIMALS are organisms made up of many cells. Living things differ from nonliving things such as ROCKS in that they can grow, develop, reproduce, and react to stimuli. Each organism is adapted to its particular HABITAT and plays important roles in its ECOSYSTEM.

Overgrazing ⚘ GRASSLANDS provide food for grazing animals such as cattle, sheep, and goats. When too many animals feed in an area, they often eat too many PLANTS and the plants die. Plant ROOTS hold water and SOIL in place. When many plants die, the land becomes bare. This can lead to severe EROSION, which can turn a grassland into a DESERT. The

release of INVASIVE SPECIES can lead to overgrazing. For example, rabbits introduced into Australia in the 1850s quickly devastated grasslands, leaving NATIVE SPECIES without food. [*See also* DESERTIFICATION.]

Oxygen ⚘

A colorless, odorless gas in the EARTH's ATMOSPHERE. Oxygen is part of a vital NUTRIENT CYCLE that moves the gas from the air to living beings and back again.

Most organisms need oxygen for cell respiration, a process in which the body breaks down sugars and releases energy that the cells can use as a fuel. Carbon dioxide and water are given off as waste materials during cell respiration.

Aquatic ANIMALS use structures called *gills* to remove oxygen from their watery surroundings. Most animals living on land use lungs to get oxygen. PLANTS and many other organisms get the oxygen they need by simply absorbing it through their cell walls and membranes. Plants give off oxygen during PHOTOSYNTHESIS, which is the process they use to make food from sunlight, water, and carbon dioxide. Photosynthesis continuously renews the supply of oxygen in the atmosphere.

Ozone ⚘

A gas found in the ATMOSPHERE. Near the ground, ozone is a pollutant that harms PLANTS, damages the eyes and lungs of ANIMALS, and destroys rubber and plastic materials. Ozone adds a sharp odor to some forms of smog.

In the upper atmosphere, ozone forms a protective layer surrounding the EARTH that filters out harmful ultraviolet light rays from sunlight. However, scientists have discovered a hole in the ozone layer over Antarctica that gets bigger each year.

The ozone hole is partly caused by CHLOROFLUOROCARBONS (CFCs), a group of chemical compounds used in refrigerators, air conditioners, and certain other materials. CFCs release chlorine into the air, where it breaks down ozone and reduces the amount of it in the atmosphere. The use and release of CFCs was banned in 1996, but it will be a long time before the CFCs already in the atmosphere are gone. Until then, they continue to destroy ozone. [*See also* AIR POLLUTION.]

Pampas ❧ *See* TEMPERATE GRASS-LANDS.

Pangea ❧ A super-continent that is thought to have formed about 250 million years ago when major landmasses collided and joined together as the result of PLATE TECTONICS. The formation of Pangea brought about major changes in land forms, CLIMATE, OCEAN depth, and OCEAN CURRENTS. The formation of Pangea also brought together many SPECIES from different regions of the EARTH. Many species became extinct, while others were able to adapt to new HABITATS. About 180 million years ago Pangea began to break into several smaller landmasses, separating many PLANTS and ANIMAL groups. Today's CONTINENTS are the result of a continuing movement of major landmasses on the earth's surface.

Parasites ❧ ORGANISMS that live in or on other living creatures, known as *hosts*. Although parasites are harmful, they usually do not kill their hosts, at least not at first. They get nutrients from the host's body. This weakens the host and makes it more vulnerable to disease. Parasites are smaller than their hosts. Most are in one of these groups: viruses, BACTERIA, FUNGI, protozoans (one-celled organisms), WORMS, and INSECTS. A plant or animal POPULATION can become filled with sick and dying individuals when it is heavily infested with parasites. Parasites can harm human populations, wildlife populations, and agricultural crops.

Parrots ❧ Small to medium-size BIRDS with stout hooked bills and fleshy tongues. Most parrots live in TROPICAL regions. Parrots, who often have brilliant colors, are very social animals. In captivity, some SPECIES learn to imitate human speech and other sounds. Unfortunately, parrots are among the most threatened and endangered of any large group of birds due to HABITAT LOSS and other

Found in tropical regions, parrots are among the most colorful animal species. Many are threatened by the destruction of their habitats and by the wildlife trade.

threats. [*See also* ENDANGERED AND THREATENED SPECIES; WILDLIFE TRADE.]

Pelagic 🌿 *See* MARINE BIOMES.

Permafrost 🌿 A layer of permanently frozen ground found in the TUNDRA. Permafrost causes a kind of drought for tundra PLANTS, because frozen water cannot be used for PHOTOSYNTHESIS. Permafrost varies in depth and thickness depending on local CLIMATE AND WEATHER conditions. Cycles of freezing and thawing

of the permafrost break apart tundra SOILS.

Pesticides 🌿 Chemicals used to control ORGANISMS that cause human diseases and destroy farm crops. Pesticides are also used to control pests such as dandelions and Japanese beetles found in lawns and gardens. There are different types of pesticides. Herbicides kill unwanted PLANTS called *weeds*. Insecticides are used to eliminate INSECTS such as ANTS, wasps, mosquitoes, fleas, and lice. Fungicides are used to get rid of unwelcome FUNGI such as molds and yeast.

Pesticides have helped humans remain healthier, grow more foods,

Pesticides help control pests that can destroy crops, but they also can pollute the environment and cause great damage if used too much or unwisely.

and have nicer-looking yards. But they are pollutants that can damage the ENVIRONMENT. These poisonous chemicals can build up in the SOIL, and they can enter GROUNDWATER, lakes, streams, and OCEANS. Pesticides also enter FOOD CHAINS AND WEBS, getting into plants and the creatures that eat them, sometimes causing great harm.

Pesticides have the potential to cause great damage. As a result, scientists are looking for ways to use natural PREDATORS instead of chemical pesticides to get rid of unwanted plants and insects. [*See also* POLLUTION; WATER POLLUTION.]

Photosynthesis

A process by which PLANTS produce their own food in the form of sugars and starches. Plants use the energy from sunlight to combine carbon dioxide and water to form sugars called *glucose*. Plants then use glucose and other sugars to form larger molecules called *starches*. OXYGEN is given off during photosynthesis, which is essential to ECOSYSTEMS because it provides food and energy for plants and for CONSUMERS that eat the plants. With rare exceptions, ANIMALS could not live without the food produced through photosynthesis. [*See also* NUTRIENT CYCLE.]

Phytoplankton

See PLANKTON.

Plankton

Small, aquatic creatures such as ALGAE, diatoms, and protozoans floating in OCEANS and in FRESHWATER BIOMES. Plankton move along with water currents, but some move up and down in the water at regular times of the day. There are two types of plankton: phytoplankton and zooplankton.

Phytoplankton are tiny floating plants found on and near the surface of the water. They are important PRODUCERS in both marine and freshwater HABITATS. Zooplankton are microscopic to small ANIMALS found throughout the pelagic zone, the area near the ocean surface. [*See also* MARINE BIOMES.]

Plants

Green ORGANISMS that produce their own food from sunlight, water, and carbon dioxide in a process called PHOTOSYNTHESIS. Plant cells contain a green pigment called *chlorophyll* that is used to capture the energy in sunlight needed for photosynthesis. During photosynthesis, plants give off, or release, much of the OXYGEN found in Earth's ATMOSPHERE. Plants are important PRODUCERS in most ECOSYSTEMS.

Most plants are rooted in the ground and must get the nutrients, water, and minerals they need from the SOIL. Rainfall, temperature, and amount of sunlight are important to the well-being of plants.

Plants are the foundation of almost every ecosystem, and there are many kinds of plants. The simplest are phytoplankton, which are tiny, one-celled, organisms that float in water. ALGAE range in size from one-celled organisms to huge seaweeds called *kelps*. Phytoplankton and algae are found in both FRESHWATER BIOMES and MARINE BIOMES. MOSSES and FERNS are plants generally found in shady and moist HABITATS. Other land plants fall into two main groups. The coniferous trees have needle-shaped leaves and seeds in cones. The second group, flowering plants, have flowers that are used to produce seeds. GRASSES, garden flowers, cacti, shrubs, and broadleaf trees are all flowering plants. [*See also* PLANKTON; ROOTS; SEED DISPERSAL; TRANSPIRATION; TREES AND SHRUBS.]

Plate Tectonics 🌱 The EARTH'S crust is broken into six to seven enormous pieces and about 24 smaller chunks called *tectonic plates*. Scientists think some of these plates were once joined together to form a single giant CONTINENT called PANGEA.

Tectonic plates float and move around on top of a layer of fluid, molten ROCKS found in a region of earth's interior called the *mantle*. The plates move an average of 3 inches (6 centimeters) a year. Large-scale tectonic plate movements, called *continental drift*, appear to have pulled Pangea apart over millions of years to form Earth's continents. Some movements pull the tectonic plates apart, forming ridges and VOLCANOES. Other movements cause plates to slide past one another, to hit each other, or to slide under one an-

Humans rely on plants for food. One of the most important plant foods in Asia is rice, which is often grown in small fields cut into the slopes of hills.

other. Tectonic plate movements cause EARTHQUAKES, are involved in the formation of MOUNTAINS, and result in volcanic eruptions. Over time, landmasses may move to different climate areas. As a result of PLATE TECTONICS, the face of the Earth is always changing.

Polar Regions See PAGE 84.

Pollination
An important part of reproduction in many PLANTS. It occurs between plants of the same SPECIES. Pollination occurs when either WIND or ANIMALS move pollen grains from male plant parts called *anthers* to female structures called *stigmas*. Pollen grains contain the male cells needed to fertilize eggs, which then develop into seeds surrounded by fruits. Cross-pollination occurs when pollen is transferred from one plant to another. In self-pollination, pollen moves from one flower to another on the same plant.

Pollution
The release of harmful substances into the air, water, or SOIL. Humans cause most pollution by adding too much of a natural material, such as the nitrogen in fertilizers, to the ENVIRONMENT, or by releasing small amounts of toxic, or poisonous, substances. Pollution harms the health, survival, and activities of both humans and wildlife. It

Smog is a form of air pollution that affects many large cities, among them Los Angeles.

also makes NATURAL RESOURCES, such as water, less usable.

A pollutant may be degradable or broken down by natural processes. Degradable substances may cause problems if they build up in the environment. For example, human sewage is normally broken down by BACTERIA and FUNGI. But sewage can pollute waterways if not handled properly by water treatment plants.

Nondegradable pollutants are not broken down naturally and can build up in the environment. Common examples of such pollutants are aluminum soda cans, disposable diapers, and plastics. Mercury, lead, and asbestos are three toxic, nondegradable pollutants that cause serious human health problems.

(continues on p. 86)

Polar Regions ⚘ Ice-covered ends of the EARTH known as the Arctic and Antarctic. These regions both have cold, harsh conditions.

Regions and Climate. The Arctic region is a large, ice-covered OCEAN near the northern edges of North America, Greenland, Europe, and Asia. It surrounds the North Pole. Subarctic waters (those close to the Arctic), support many living creatures. These areas have less ice and are a little warmer and much richer in the nutrients that ORGANISMS need to live and grow. The subarctic waters are very important to humans because they support about one-tenth of all commercial fishing.

The Antarctic surrounds the South Pole. It is made up of a large unfrozen ocean and a mostly ice-covered CONTINENT about twice as large as Australia. The Antarctic has a huge ice sheet about 8,000 feet (2,500 meters) thick. Because the coastal areas of the continent are warmed by OCEAN CURRENTS, a greater diversity of PLANTS and ANIMALS live in these areas. The Antarctic Peninsula is a slender piece of land that stretches toward the southern tip of South America. It has a milder climate than the rest of the region, and its plants are similar to those of the TUNDRA.

Plants. Not many PLANTS can survive polar conditions. There are only 400 plant SPECIES in the Antarc-

Penguins are found only in the southern hemisphere. These emperor penguins are well adapted to their polar environment.

Key Species: Penguins

Found only in the southern hemisphere, penguins are BIRDS that spend most of their lives at sea. They come on shore only to mate and bring up their young. Penguins have lost the ability to fly. But they have many ADAPTATIONS for swimming, diving, and surviving in cold areas.

There are 17 penguin SPECIES. Eleven are either endangered, threatened, or considered vulnerable to future decreases in their POPULATIONS. Loss of breeding HABITAT because of human land use is a big problem for penguins. Human fishermen also compete with penguins for food and often catch them in their fishing nets. Oil spills also cause many penguin deaths.

tic. Among them are MOSSES and liverworts, which form carpet-like patches in coastal areas. Other plant forms include ALGAE and LICHENS.

Animals. WORMS, mites, small flying INSECTS called midges, and tiny insects named springtails are some of the very few INVERTEBRATES found on the ice in polar regions. Large populations of krill, or shrimp-like PLANKTON, live in the cold polar waters. VERTEBRATES found in polar regions include fish, polar bears (along the coasts of the Arctic), and the penguins and other BIRDS that use the Antarctic to form large breeding colonies.

Human Impact. Humans have damaged and disrupted the polar regions in a number of ways. Oil spills have caused widespread environmental problems and killed FISH, penguins, seabirds, seals, and other animals. The mining of minerals on the Antarctic continent may lead to further harm in the form of HABITAT destruction and POLLUTION.

Overhunting by humans has greatly reduced natural POPULATIONS of polar animals such as fur seals, elephant seals, blue whales, and fin whales. Antarctic krill are harvested in large numbers, reducing food supplies for cold water sea animals.

Perhaps of greatest concern is global warming, a rise in air and water temperatures around the world. Higher global temperatures may lead to large-scale melting of polar ice masses. This would release freshwater into the oceans and possibly cause flooding in coastal regions throughout the world. [*See also* GREENHOUSE EFFECT.]

Biome Snapshot: Polar Regions

Geographical Regions: Northern and southern ice-covered regions of the Earth. **Climate:** Harsh, cold, and very windy conditions. The Antarctic averages below-freezing temperatures all year long; Antarctica winter temperatures average –40°F to –94°F (–40°C to –70°C); lowest temperature recorded was –129°F (–89.6°C). The Arctic is a frozen ocean, but most of the surrounding waters are above freezing (32°F, 0°C). **Precipitation:** Less than 11.8 inches (30 centimeters) of annual rainfall in the Antarctic. **Seasons and Daylight:** Long, dark winters followed by short summers; Antarctic islands have somewhat milder seasons, with cool, wet summers and winters. **Dominant Plant Life:** When present, includes algae, liverworts, lichens and moss. **Dominant Animal Life:** Mostly aquatic, or semi-aquatic; krill and fish, which serve as food for seals, whales, penguins, and other birds; polar bears found along the coasts of the Arctic. Penguins and other birds use the Antarctic to form large breeding colonies.

(continued from p. 83)

Pollution is a bigger problem in areas with large human POPULATIONS. One way to reduce the world's pollution problems is to slow human population growth. RECYCLING programs, cleaner and more efficient manufacturing processes, and laws controlling industrial wastes are other ways to ease pollution problems. [*See also* AIR POLLUTION; HAZARDOUS WASTE; SUSTAINABLE DEVELOPMENT; WATER POLLUTION.]

Population ⚘ A group of ORGANISMS belonging to the same SPECIES and living in the same area or region. The members of a population often share resources, experience similar conditions, and compete with one another for mates, shelter, and food.

To look at the impact of a population on NATURAL RESOURCES, scientists consider various factors, including individuals in an area, their distribution, and whether the population is getting bigger or smaller. No population can grow unchecked. In nature, most populations stop growing when they begin to run out of resources like food and space, or when they fall prey to PREDATORS or disease.

Human populations grew very slowly until about 500 years ago, when there were only about 500 million humans on EARTH. By October

Case Study: Overpopulation in China

In the past, China's population has gone through cycles of growth and declines related to large food shortages called *famines*, natural disasters, and widespread starvation. Between 1950 and 1980, China's death rate went down, while the average age at death increased. The result was a rapid increase in population size. By 1995 the Chinese population had grown to 1,238 million people, about 22 percent of all humans on earth.

The Chinese government now has strict rules limiting families to just one child. As a result, birth rates have dropped. Couples who sign a pledge to have only one child get better housing, more money, and promises of special schools and jobs for their child. While this program has caused some difficult social problems, it has been very effective in controlling population growth and improving conditions for the Chinese people.

1999 the human population had reached an astounding 6 billion people. Earth's human population is now rapidly using up NATURAL RESOURCES, increasing POLLUTION, and causing physical damage to global ECOSYSTEMS. [*See also* NICHE.]

Prairies ⚘ *See* TEMPERATE GRASSLANDS.

Precipitation ⚑

Rain, snow, sleet, ICE, fog, and dew. Precipitation plays a major role in the WATER CYCLE. It is also an important part of an area's CLIMATE AND WEATHER and can determine which PLANTS and ANIMALS can live there. It is one of the defining environmental conditions for each of the world's BIOMES. Rain and snow patterns vary depending on a region's climate, air currents, and EVAPORATION rates. Warm and dry air over DESERTS increase evaporation and leave less water in the air for precipitation. In some TROPICAL regions, precipitation only occurs during rainy seasons. In other regions, rain is fairly constant all year.

In subtropical areas, seasonal rains called *monsoons* bring heavy downpours that often cause flooding.

Predators ⚑

CARNIVORES such as spiders, lions, and SHARKS that kill other live animals for food. Cannibals are predators that sometimes eat members of their own SPECIES. Some predators, like dogs and lions, are known as *general predators*. They feed on many different kinds of prey, eating whatever type is most abundant and easiest to catch. *Specialized predators* eat only one or two kinds of prey. Predators are important members of an ECOSYSTEM because they often control the size of prey POPULATIONS, preventing them from exhausting their food supply. However, if predators consume too many of the same species, they can threaten the survival of that species. [*See also* FOOD CHAINS AND WEBS.]

Producers ⚑

ORGANISMS that capture energy from the ENVIRONMENT and use it to produce food. CONSUMERS depend on producers for food to eat. Producers are usually PLANTS that use a process called PHOTOSYNTHESIS to make food from sunlight, carbon dioxide, and water. All BIOMES are fueled by the energy that producers capture from the environment. This energy is passed on to animal consumers when they eat plants.

Public Lands ⚑

Land held by local, state, or federal governments for the

benefit of their citizens. In the United States, about 40 percent of all land is owned by the government. Most of these public lands are in Alaska and the western states. Government agencies manage public lands, using them to protect wildlife, for human recreational activities, as grazing lands, and for mineral development. American public lands have been divided into NATIONAL PARKS, national FORESTS, WILDLIFE REFUGES, and other types of natural reserves. [*See also* NATURAL RESOURCES.]

Rainforests ⚜ *See* TROPICAL FORESTS.

Recycling ⚜ A natural process or human activity in which a resource is reprocessed to use again. Natural recycling is a process in nature that occurs when wastes are broken down through DECOMPOSITION. This releases nutrients that can then be reused by ORGANISMS. Many ECOSYSTEMS, such as MARSHES, help clean up pollutants by absorbing and destroying harmful substances. The WATER CYCLE is also a natural recycling process that helps cleanse water resources.

Humans often waste resources by throwing things away as garbage. Reducing the amount and kinds of garbage we produce and recycling

Recycling waste materials helps conserve resources and protect the environment.

materials would greatly benefit the ENVIRONMENT. Industries that recycle paper and metals help reduce the amount of waste sent to landfills. Companies can also help reduce waste by using less cardboard, plastic, and plastic wrap to package products.

Most garbage is sent to landfills, which quickly become filled up and may harm the surrounding environment. To reduce the amount of material in landfills, people can send newspapers, magazines, cardboard, metal, glass, and many plastics to local recycling programs. [*See also* NUTRIENT CYCLES; WASTE MANAGEMENT.]

Redwoods ⚘ Huge evergreen trees growing in the cool, moist FORESTS of the western United States. Found in OLD-GROWTH FORESTS, redwoods may live 3,000 to 4,000 years. There are two SPECIES of redwoods: redwood trees and giant sequoias. Redwood trees grow to 385 feet (117 meters) tall and have trunks 10 to 25 feet (3 to 7.6 meters) around. These trees live in valleys near the coasts of Washington, Oregon, and California. Giant sequoias grow to 325 feet (99 meters) tall and have trunks 10 to 30 feet (3 to 9.1 meters) around. This species of redwood is found only in California, on the slopes of the Sierra Nevada mountains. Humans have cut down many of these ancient trees for lumber. Most remaining old-growth redwood trees grow in protected reserves. [*See also* NATIONAL PARKS; TREES AND SHRUBS.]

Reptiles ⚘ VERTEBRATES with dry, scaly skin. Turtles, lizards, SNAKES, and alligators are all reptiles. Most reptiles are CARNIVORES, but some are HERBIVORES or OMNIVORES. Most reptiles are adapted for life on land, using lungs to breathe. Some types of sea snakes and turtles spend much of the time in water, but they come to the surface to breathe.

Reptiles are described as being COLD-BLOODED, which means that their body temperature varies ac-

Many reptiles, such as snakes, play an important role in the environment by controlling populations of insects, rats, and other animals.

cording to the temperature of their surrounding ENVIRONMENT. But many reptiles actually keep about the same body temperature by moving into the sun to warm up and into shadier areas to cool off.

Dinosaurs were the dominant vertebrates on EARTH for millions of years before going extinct. Some scientists think BIRDS have evolved from those ancient reptiles. In fact, some scientists think of birds as a special kind of reptile.

Resources ⚘ *See* NATURAL RESOURCES.

Restoration Ecology ⚘ The study and practice of returning damaged local POPULATIONS or HABI-

TATS to nearly natural states. Restoration ecology involves trying to create exactly the same population or habitat that was once native to an area. For example, there have been widely publicized attempts to return wolves to their original habitats in parts of the United States. Restoration ecology also involves efforts to rebuild whole PLANT and ANIMAL communities destroyed by strip mining, by draining salt MARSHES, and by draining and filling other WETLANDS. When a complete restoration is not possible, scientists try to rehabilitate the area by bringing in plant and animal SPECIES with traits that are similar to those that have been lost, both in terms of their effect on the ENVIRONMENT and in their value to humans.

Trying to repair the harm that humans have caused to ECOSYSTEMS is not always successful. It is often too difficult and complicated to undo the damage caused by EROSION, deforestation, OVERGRAZING, DESERTIFICATION, mining, and other factors that alter natural landscapes. Restoration is more likely to be successful when it is done early. [*See also* SUSTAINABLE DEVELOPMENT.]

Riparian Environments ⚘ *See* FRESHWATER BIOMES.

Rivers ⚘ *See* FRESHWATER BIOMES.

Rocks ⚘ Hard, stony material that forms part of the EARTH. Rocks are made up of two or more minerals, or chemical compounds. There are three kinds of rocks. Igneous rocks are

Rocky landscapes, such as this area in Iceland, are found in many places on Earth.

made of cooled material from the hot, molten material under the Earth's crust. Sedimentary rocks are either pieces of larger rocks or matter that was once dissolved in liquid. Metamorphic rocks are formed by heat, physical forces, or chemical reactions. The gradual breakdown of rocks by rain, WIND, waves, or GLACIERS is known as *weathering*. This process is essential to the creation of SOIL.

Roots ☙ Parts of PLANTS that collect nutrients from SOIL, air, or water. The roots of most plants reach down into the soil. These roots help to anchor a plant in the ground. They also soak up nutrients, minerals, and water, which plants need to grow and survive. The roots of some plants called EPIPHYTES hang in the air, while the roots of floating plants dangle in the water. Soil-based roots play an important role in maintaining ECOSYSTEMS by helping to prevent soil EROSION. [*See also* TRANSPIRATION; TROPICAL FORESTS.]

Runoff ☙ Part of the WATER CYCLE. Runoff is water from rain, ICE, and snow that does not evaporate or soak into the ground but flows downhill into lakes, streams, and ponds. Runoff sometimes causes EROSION, which shapes the surface of the land. It also picks up and carries fertilizers, PESTICIDES, and other forms of POLLUTION into streams and lakes. Runoff combines with stream and river water to empty into the OCEANS. [*See also* DESERTIFICATION; FRESHWATER BIOMES; WATER POLLUTION.]

Savannas ❧ *See* TROPICAL GRASS-LANDS.

Scavengers ❧ ANIMALS that eat dead or dying ORGANISMS, body wastes, rotting leaves and logs, and overripe fruit. Crayfish are the most common freshwater INVERTEBRATE scavengers. Other invertebrate scavengers include some INSECTS, especially BEETLES and flies. Large scavenging BIRDS such as vultures often have bare heads and necks, which makes it easier to get cleaned up after sticking their beaks into dead animals. Gulls and crows are scavenging birds that often eat garbage. Scavenging MAMMALS include hyenas, jackals, and sometimes lions. [*See also* DECOMPOSITION; FOOD CHAINS AND WEBS; TROPHIC LEVEL.]

Scrublands ❧ Dry areas generally found along the coast of California, in the Mediterranean region, and in parts of South Africa and Australia. A type of scrubland called desert GRASSLAND is found around the edges of DESERTS in Mexico, Arizona, New Mexico, and Texas.

Most scrublands have short shrubs or bushes such as the creosote bush. Scrubland shrubs are often spiny and have hard leaves covered

Areas of scrubland usually contain only short bushes and shrubs. This scrubland is in Sandy Hook, New Jersey.

with a waxy material that prevents water loss. They often have long ROOTS that grow into the ground in search of water. Scrubland areas with mild, wet winters and dry summers have a variety of green PLANTS, and some even have small TREES.

Seas ⚘ See MARINE BIOMES; OCEANS.

Seashores ⚘ See COASTLINES.

Seasons ⚘ Divisions of the year based on regular changes in CLIMATE AND WEATHER. DESERTS and TROPI-

Some areas of the world have four very distinct seasons, including a colorful autumn, when leaves turn different colors before falling off trees.

CAL FORESTS have relatively little seasonal change. Some tropical regions and SCRUBLANDS have two seasons: a hot, dry season followed by a rainy season. TEMPERATE regions experience four seasons. Local conditions may vary, but the general seasonal pattern in temperate regions is to have cold winters with short days and long nights. This is followed by the longer days and warmer weather of spring. Then come the long days, short nights, and even warmer weather of summer, followed by shorter days and cooler weather in the fall. [*See also* PRECIPITATION.]

Sedges ⚘ PLANTS that look like GRASSES but are not. Sedges have long, slender leaves that resemble large blades of grass. When the stem of a sedge is cut in half, it looks like a triangle. Sedge blades grow in clumps. The plants live around the edges of ponds, in MARSHES, and along rivers. Sedge ROOTS grow in wet, muddy water. Their stems and blades reach up over the surface of ponds, marshes, or rivers. In BOGS, sedges and sphagnum MOSS form floating mats. [*See also* WETLANDS.]

Seed Dispersal ⚘ The movement of seeds, or scattering, away from a parent PLANT. Seed dispersal is important because it determines where

a young plant will have to try to grow. It has a better chance if it does not have to compete with its parent for light and nutrients. Seeds are dispersed in many ways. Winds carry some seeds, such as dandelion seeds, while water moves coconuts. BIRDS and bats often eat fruit seeds, which are then released with the animal's body wastes far from the parent plant. Other seeds, such as thistles, have hooks or barbs that catch on passing ANIMALS, which can carry them long distances.

Sharks and Rays ⚘ Fast-swimming fish that live in MARINE BIOMES. Sharks and rays are VERTEBRATES with skeletons made of cartilage, a material that is softer than bone. Sharks and rays are important CARNIVORES in their HABITATS. Rays use strong jaws and teeth to crush snails, oysters, and other INVERTEBRATES. Sharks also have strong jaws and sharp, pointy teeth that they use to catch and eat prey.

Sierra Club ⚘ *See* CONSERVATION ORGANIZATIONS.

Smog ⚘ *See* AIR POLLUTION.

Snakes ⚘ Legless members of the VERTEBRATE class of REPTILES. Most snakes live on the ground, but some burrow in the SOIL or climb TREES. Sea snakes spend their lives in water. Snakes are found throughout many of the EARTH's warmer regions. Some are also found in colder regions. Snakes are CARNIVORES, eating many different kinds of prey, from INSECTS to AMPHIBIANS to small MAMMALS. They are very sensitive to chemicals given off by prey. They also sense ground vibrations caused by the movements of other animals. Some snakes, such as rattlesnakes and cobras, inject poisons into their prey through sharp, hollow teeth, or fangs. Many snakes can open their mouths very wide to swallow mice and rats whole.

Soil ⚘ A relatively shallow layer of material atop the EARTH's crust, generally ranging from a few inches to several feet thick. Soil contains small mineral particles formed by the weathering, or breakdown, of larger ROCKS. These particles make up the sand, silt, clay, and small stones found in soil. Soils differ based on the amount of sand, silt, and clay they contain. PLANTS need the right amounts of air, water, and nutrients in the soils to grow and be healthy.

Soil contains many living ORGANISMS. BACTERIA, FUNGI, and other MICROORGANISMS all make their homes in the soil. These organisms

The age-old agricultural technique of plowing helps crop plants take root but can lead to erosion and exhaustion of the soil.

work as decomposers, breaking down decaying matter from wastes and dead organisms. Many INVERTEBRATES live in the soil, including earthworms and roundworms. Such invertebrates are part of soil FOOD CHAINS, and they often play important roles in NUTRIENT CYCLES.

An area's soil can be destroyed when humans cut down TREES and when RUNOFF and strong WINDS cause EROSION. Soil can also be ruined by POLLUTION, especially when petroleum leaks from gas station tanks, and when fertilizers are overused. [*See also* DESERTIFICATION.]

Solar Energy ⚘ *See* ENERGY SOURCES; SUN.

Speciation ⚘ The evolution of new SPECIES, often as a result of NATURAL SELECTION. Most speciation occurs when some members of a POPULATION become separated from the rest by a large barrier such as a MOUNTAIN or an OCEAN. While alone, the separated population begins to develop new features, or ADAPTATIONS, that help them live in the new ENVIRONMENT. If the separated population lives apart from the original population for a number of LIFE CYCLES, or generations, the two may become very different from one another. Speciation has occurred when the two populations have lost the ability to mate or produce young with one another. [*See also* EVOLUTION AND EXTINCTION.]

Species and Subspecies ⚘ A species is a group of ORGANISMS that can mate with one another to produce young. Members of a species share traits such as size, color, and behavior. They are generally found in similar HABITATS. Most important, the members of a species share ADAPTATIONS that help them survive in certain ENVIRONMENTS.

Scientists have identified about 1.4 million species of PLANTS, ANIMALS, and other organisms so far. Habitat destruction, POLLUTION, and over-harvesting of natural POPULA-

TIONS are all contributing to the loss of many precious species.

A subspecies is a smaller population within a species that has developed so many adaptations to a local environment that its members are distinctly different from the rest of the species. Despite the differences, however, the subspecies is still able to mate with the rest of the species and produce young. [*See also* NICHE; SPECIATION.]

Species Interactions ⚘ A term used to describe how two SPECIES

Case Study: Hummingbird Bills

An example of a species interaction that leads to coevolution involves hummingbirds and the flowers from which they drink nectar. Hummingbirds carry pollen from flower to flower as they eat. They depend on the flowers for their food. The PLANTS depend on the hummingbirds to pollinate their flowers. Over time many hummingbird species have evolved bills that are just the right size and shape to fit into the flowers from which they sip nectar. This makes it easier for hummingbirds to pick up pollen from one flower and leave it on the next flower they visit, and it helps to ensure that the flowers will be pollinated successfully.

that live in the same area can directly influence each other. Some examples of species interactions are: PREDATORS and their prey; PARASITES and their hosts; MUTUALISM; and PLANTS and the ANIMALS that pollinate their flowers.

Species interactions can lead to *coevolution*, a process in which both species develop new traits in response to each other. For example, plants may produce chemicals that make them taste bad to the HERBIVORES that eat their leaves or fruit. The herbivores, in turn, evolve the ability to break down the chemicals so that they can eat the plants. You may recognize some chemicals made by plants to stop herbivores. They include cinnamon, cloves, and peppermint. [*See also* ADAPTATION; EVOLUTION AND EXTINCTION; POLLINATION.]

Species Loss ⚘ *See* EVOLUTION AND EXTINCTION; HABITAT LOSS.

Steppes ⚘ *See* TEMPERATE GRASSLANDS.

Streams ⚘ *See* FRESHWATER BIOMES.

Succession ⚘ Natural changes in the number and kinds of SPECIES in a community over a very long time. Succession often begins with just a few species and ends with a stable,

Case Study: Mount St. Helens

On May 18, 1980, Mount St. Helens in the state of Washington erupted violently. The eruption caused a massive landslide that swept away and buried ancient FORESTS. Most PLANTS and ANIMALS in the immediate area were killed when they were covered by volcanic ash and debris.

This devastating natural disaster gave scientists a chance to study succession. They were surprised to find that succession in the area around Mount St. Helens did not always go from pioneering stages to climax communities as expected. Instead, all stages of the forest began to grow at the same time.

For example, pioneer SPECIES often have a very difficult time invading volcanic ash because it has no soil and very little nutrients. However, soon after Mount St. Helens erupted, pocket gophers began digging tunnels, which brought up rich soil and buried seeds that quickly sprouted to form new PLANTS. A plant called *fireweed* also quickly reached fertile soil under the volcanic ash by sending out long ROOTS, and it was soon producing bright pink flowers. Elk and other HERBIVORES also returned to the area sooner than expected, and their POPULATIONS grew along with the plants.

long-lasting community of many different species. Such a community is called a *climax community*.

On land, succession starts in a new or recently disturbed HABITAT with dry, bare ground, little or no SOIL, and no protection from the SUN and WIND. Invading pioneer species, also called colonizers, have ADAPTATIONS that allow them to live under these conditions. LICHENS, MOSSES, and some flying INSECTS are often pioneer species. Pioneer species also tend to quickly fill up open habitats by having a lot of young. As the POPULATION grows, what was once a sunny, hot, and dry habitat often becomes shadier, cooler, and moister. The SOIL is also enriched when their dead bodies are broken down through DECOMPOSITION.

Pioneer species cannot tolerate these changes and are slowly replaced by species adapted for the new conditions. Over many years the habitat fills with a variety of other species. A climax community has reached a place where the conditions and the number of species are stable or no longer change very much. Two familiar North American climax communities are beech-maple and oak-hickory FORESTS.

Sun ☙ The star at the center of our solar system, around which the EARTH and the eight other planets revolve. The Sun, like other stars, is a huge ball of burning gas that releases

enormous amounts of energy in the form of light and heat. This energy provides the starting point for PHOTOSYNTHESIS by PLANTS and are the basis for the Earth's CLIMATE. It is the energy of the Sun that makes all life on Earth possible.

Sustainable Development

The intelligent and responsible development, management, and use of NATURAL RESOURCES. An important part of sustainable development involves harvesting or using only so much of a natural resource. The idea is to allow each resource enough time to be renewed, or returned to its original state, before being collected or harvested again.

Sustainable development also involves trying to find ways to slow our use of resources before they are completely depleted. For example, sustainable development of a FOREST would involve removing only a few TREES as lumber and then not disturbing the forest again until those trees had been fully replaced.

Sustainable development benefits both humans and wildlife. People can continue to use technology and other advances while enjoying fresh air, pure water, and unpolluted land and waterways. At the same time, wildlife is protected from destructive activities that degrade or damage their HABITATS.

Successful sustainable development requires learning about how ECOSYSTEMS work, especially the ways in which BIOLOGICAL DIVERSITY and SPECIES INTERACTIONS support the continued well-being of natural processes. [*See also* RESTORATION ECOLOGY.]

Swamps

Areas of land having water on or above the surface. A swamp is a type of WETLAND where TREES AND SHRUBS grow. PLANTS adapted to living in a swamp must be able to survive with their ROOTS under water for all or part of the year. Swamps in different regions often have their own distinct plant SPECIES. For example, bald cypress trees are often found in southeastern swamps.

Swamps provide HABITATS for many kinds of ANIMALS, including various species of MAMMALS. BIRDS, AMPHIBIANS, REPTILES, and INSECTS. In the southeast United States, for example, swamps are home to the once-endangered American alligator, egrets, bullfrogs, owls, cranes, bobcats, skinks, bears, and rattlesnakes.

Symbiosis

See MUTUALISM.

Taiga ❧ *See* BOREAL FORESTS.

Temperate ❧ Areas that experience cold winters and warm summers, found between the TROPICS and the POLAR REGIONS in the Northern and Southern Hemispheres. Temperate areas usually have four SEASONS, with moderate temperatures. TEMPERATE BROADLEAF FORESTS and TEMPERATE GRASSLANDS are the major BIOMES found in the temperate zones. [*See also* CLIMATE AND WEATHER.]

Temperate Broadleaf Forests
❧ *See* PAGE 100.

Temperate Grasslands ❧ *See* PAGE 102.

Temperature ❧ *See* CLIMATE AND WEATHER.

Termites ❧ INSECTS with small, soft bodies and narrow wings that live together in large nests, or colonies. Termites are social ANIMALS and have distinct groups in their colonies, including queens, kings, workers, and soldiers. The kings and queens reproduce young, the workers look for food for the colony, and the soldiers guard the nest.

Termites eat wood, but they cannot digest it without the help of microscopic creatures called *protozoa* that live in their stomachs and break down the wood. The relationship between the protozoa and the termites is an example of MUTUALISM.

Termites are a dominant SPECIES in tropical and temperate BIOMES. They play an important role in DECOMPOSITION. An important food source for many animals, termites may affect the global CLIMATE through the production of methane gas. When released into the ATMOSPHERE, this gas contributes to the GREENHOUSE EFFECT.

Thermal Vents ❧ Hot springs deep in the OCEANS where there are cracks in the sea floor. Seawater seeps into these cracks and comes in contact with the hot magma, or melted ROCK, *(continues on p. 104)*

Temperate Broadleaf Forests

☙ Forests found in regions where rain or other forms of PRECIPITATION fall year round, winters are generally cold, and PLANTS only grow during the warmer months of the year. The main characteristic of these forests is that they contain primarily broadleaf TREES, also called *deciduous trees*, which lose their leaves in the winter and grow new ones in the spring.

The dominant plants in temperate broadleaf forests are deciduous trees, which lose their leaves in the fall and grow new ones in the spring.

Key Species: Oaks

Among the most important trees on EARTH, oaks are the dominant PLANTS in some temperate broadleaf FORESTS. Between 50 and 75 oak species grow in the United States, mostly in the eastern part of the country. Oaks are large trees that form a canopy, or layer of leaves, that shades the ground. Oaks are well known for their fruits, called *acorns*. Forest deer, squirrels, and raccoons all depend on acorns for food. Humans use oak trees for lumber, fuel, and railroad ties.

Regions. The world's TEMPERATE zones lie between the TROPICS and the TUNDRA and POLAR REGIONS in the Northern Hemisphere and between the tropics and the Antarctic polar regions in the Southern Hemisphere. Temperate broadleaf forests are found in western and central Europe, eastern Asia, and the eastern United States.

Climate. Temperate broadleaf forests experience seasonal changes in temperature and precipitation. The average summer temperature is generally 75°F (24°C), or more. Temperatures fall below freezing in the winter. Summers are warm and moist, with relatively high humidity. Between 30 and 80 inches (76 to 200 centimeters) of precipitation falls each year.

Plants. These forests are known for their dense stands of broadleaf trees, such as oaks, maples, hickories, elms, and ash. The forests may also have a few coniferous trees such as pines. Shrubs, FERNS, MOSSES, and LICHENS form a dense undergrowth in the forests. Many wild flowers bloom in the spring, before the trees leaf out and shade the forest floor.

Animals. INVERTEBRATES, especially INSECTS, are common in broadleaf forests, but most are only active during the warmer months. SNAKES, turtles, FROGS, toads, and salamanders are also abundant during milder weather.

Broadleaf forests are also home to a wide variety of BIRDS, including robins, gray catbirds, northern cardinals, woodpeckers, owls, and hawks. Many small and medium-size MAMMALS, such as squirrels, chipmunks, raccoons, mice, foxes, porcupines, and opossums live in broadleaf forests. Large mammals such as deer, wolves, and black bears also make these forests their homes.

Human Impact. Humans have cut down almost all of the original broadleaf forests in North America, and even more of the natural forests in Europe. In some broadleaf forests, trees are selectively logged, which means that some trees are left standing. Some people question how many

trees can be removed without causing permanent damage to the forests. Temperate forests are also threatened by global warming and other forms of AIR POLLUTION, such as ACID RAIN. Widespread deforestation causes other environmental problems, such as EROSION, WATER POLLUTION, and DESERTIFICATION.

Biome Snapshot: Temperate Broadleaf Forests

Geographical Region: Temperate regions of the world; western and central Europe; eastern Asia; and the eastern United States. **Climate:** Temperate, seasonal climates with harsh winters and mild or even hot summers; average summer temperature 75°F (24°C), or more; high humidity. **Precipitation:** Between 30 to 80 inches (76 to 200 centimeters) per year. **Seasons:** Distinct winters, springs, summers, and falls. **Daylight:** Longer in summer, shorter in winter. **Dominant Plant Life:** Broadleaf trees that shed their leaves each year (also called deciduous trees); beech, maple, oak, and hickory trees. **Dominant Animal Life:** Insects and other invertebrates; many amphibians and reptiles; a rich diversity of birds, including robins, gray catbirds, warblers, woodpeckers, owls, and hawks; deer, bears, and wolves; many other small and medium-sized mammals such as squirrels and chipmunks.

Temperate Grasslands ⚘ Grassy

TEMPERATE regions with cold winters, hot summers, and too little rainfall for FORESTS to grow. Many temperate GRASSLANDS have been cleared for farming and grazing because of their rich SOILS and long growing season.

Regions. Temperate grasslands are found mainly in the central regions of CONTINENTS, north and south of the TROPICS. Each area has its own unique temperate grassland. Grasslands called *prairies* once covered most of central North America. In Central Russia and other Asian regions, grasslands called *steppes* are notable for having have less water than most grasslands but more than a DESERT. South American temperate grasslands, which are called *pampas*, are found in Argentina and Uruguay. Temperate grasslands called the *veldt* are found in Africa. Southern India and Northern Australia also have temperate grasslands.

Climate. These grasslands have temperate conditions, with hot and dry summers. The growing season is between 120 and 300 days long. Winters vary from mild to cold and snowy. Yearly rainfall is from 10 to 30 inches (25 to 75 centimeters).

Plants. GRASSES, wildflowers, and a few bushes dominate this BIOME. Short grasses are found in areas with less rain, while taller grasses are found in wetter locations. Seasonal drought conditions, frequent FIRES, and herds of grazing ANIMALS make it difficult for TREES AND SHRUBS to grow in temperate grasslands.

Animals. Large HERBIVORES, such as the bison, pronghorn antelope, and horse are common in North America's temperate grasslands. The African veldt is home to such herbivores as gazelles and zebra, while wild horses and sheep live in the steppes of Asia. Kangaroos are among the most common herbivores found in Australia's grasslands.

Many burrowing animals also live in grasslands, including prairie dogs, mice, voles, shrews, rabbits, skunks, badgers, and foxes. Large PREDATORS such as cheetahs, lions, and leopards are found in African

The pampas, a temperate grassland region in Argentina, contains vast fertile plains covered by grasses and farmland.

grasslands. Wolves and coyotes are found in the grassland HABITATS of North America.

Among the many BIRDS living in temperate grasslands are grouse, hawks, vultures, meadowlarks, and various sparrows. Loss of grasslands due to human activities may be the cause of the decline in many bird POPULATIONS.

Grasslands are also alive with many INSECTS, including monarch butterflies, moths, and grasshoppers. Prairie rattlesnake and box turtles are also found in this biome.

Human Impact. Temperate grasslands have some of the richest SOIL in the world. Wild grasses also provide easy grazing for farm animals. These two facts have led to a large conversion of natural grasslands worldwide into farm fields and pastures. For example, North America's once vast prairies have been reduced to small patches in protected areas and along railroad tracks. [*See also* TROPICAL GRASSLANDS.]

Key Species: Bison

The American bison, also known as the buffalo, is a large HERBIVORE adapted to cold, heat, and dry conditions. Sixty million buffalo once lived on the North American prairies. In the spring, large herds moved north, where they could graze on spring grasses. In the fall, they traveled south to avoid the snow. Plains Indians ate bison meat and used the animals' skins to build homes and make clothing. Buffalo hide was turned into saddles and ropes.

In the 1800s, pioneers moved to the prairies, and vast railroad systems were constructed. Settlers and the U.S. Army killed up to 4 million bison per year in the 1870s. By 1889 only 541 bison were left alive in North America. Laws protecting the remaining animals and the establishment of WILDLIFE REFUGES saved the SPECIES from extinction. Bison POPULATIONS have grown steadily in the past century.

Biome Snapshot: Prairies

Geographical Region: Prairies of North America; steppes of Russia and other Asian regions; pampas in Argentina and Uruguay; the veldt of Africa; large portions of India and Australia. **Climate:** Temperate, with hot and dry summers and mild to cold winters. **Precipitation:** 10 to 30 inches (25 to 75 centimeters) per year. **Seasons:** Four distinct seasons: winter, spring, summer, and fall. **Daylight:** Short days and long nights in the winter; long days and short nights in the summer. **Dominant Plant Life:** Grasses and wildflowers. **Dominant Animal Life:** Large herbivores such as bison, horses, gazelles, and zebras; burrowing animals such as mice, voles, shrews, rabbits, skunks, badgers, and foxes; grassland birds, including grouse, sparrows, and meadowlarks.

(continued from p. 99)

under the EARTH's crust. The water becomes overheated and gushes out of the cracks, carrying chemicals such as methane and iron.

Unusual marine ECOSYSTEMS are found near thermal vents, where the water is warmer than the surrounding sea water. The vents are often found in deep areas where no light can penetrate. Because there is no light, specialized BACTERIA use a process similar to PHOTOSYNTHESIS to produce food from the chemicals released by the vents. Many INVERTEBRATES near thermal vents eat these bacteria as food. Other invertebrates, rather than eating the bacteria, keep them in their bodies and use the chemicals made by them as food. [*See also* MARINE BIOMES; PLATE TECTONICS.]

Threatened Species ⚘ *See* EN- DANGERED AND THREATENED SPECIES.

Tidal Pools ⚘ *See* MARINE BIOMES.

Tides ⚘ The regular, predictable rise and fall of the water level of OCEANS and large lakes. Tides are caused by the gravitational pull of the MOON and the SUN, along with the rotation of the EARTH on its axis. Most places on Earth have two cycles of high and low tides a day. The tide height, or how far the water rises and falls, is influenced by the phase of the Moon.

Tides in the Bay of Fundy in Nova Scotia rise and fall 50 feet or more.

Various intertidal creatures live where the water rises and falls because of tides. They must be able to withstand being covered by water at high tide, and then exposed to hot, dry conditions at low tide.

Tides influence the shape of COASTLINES by moving sand and through EROSION. It is possible to harness this power using tidal power plants to generate electricity. [*See also* FRESHWATER BIOMES; MARINE BIOMES; OCEAN CURRENTS.]

Topography ⚘ The physical features and shape of the land, such as plains, hills, lakes, MOUNTAINS, and valleys. Topography affects which PLANTS and ANIMALS live in an area because it has a big impact on how much water, humidity, and light are present. Topography influences local temperatures. It also affects human ENVIRON-

MENTS. For example, deep valleys can add to smog problems by trapping AIR POLLUTION near the ground. [*See also* LANDSCAPE; PLATE TECTONICS.]

Topsoil ☙ *See* SOIL.

Transpiration
☙ A process in which water evaporates from a PLANT through tiny openings in leaves called *stomata*. Plant ROOTS soak up water from the SOIL. Transpiration helps pull water from the roots and carry it to other parts of the plant. Transpiration also plays a role in the WATER CYCLE by returning water to the ATMOSPHERE. [*See also* PHOTOSYNTHESIS.]

Treeline
☙ Also called the timberline, the elevation on MOUNTAINS beyond which trees cannot grow. The southern edge of the Arctic TUNDRA is also marked by a treeline. The location of a treeline seems to be set by average summer temperatures. If temperatures are too low for too long, trees cannot make and store enough food to survive the colder parts of the year. Snowfall and WIND also limit tree growth. Trees that grow near the treeline grow very slowly and have long lives. Bristlecone pines, found at the timberline in the mountains of the southwestern United States, may live up to 4,000 years. [*See also* TREES AND SHRUBS.]

Trees and Shrubs
☙ PLANTS with woody stems. Shrubs are relatively smaller, bushy plants with branches that form several stems. FOREST shrubs form a thick brush that serves as cover and food for many ANIMALS, especially BIRDS.

Trees are larger than shrubs. They have a single thick stem, or trunk, and branches that form a crown at the top of the tree. There are two types of trees. Coniferous trees—also called *conifers*—have needle-like leaves. Conifer seeds form in cones. Firs, pines, and spruce trees are all conifers. REDWOOD trees are huge, long-lived conifers. Deciduous, or broadleaf trees, are flowering plants with wide leaves that are shed each year. The seeds of deciduous trees are formed in flowers. Maple, oak, hickory, and fruit trees are all broadleaf trees.

Trees and shrubs are an important part of many BIOMES. They shape the physical structure of many ECOSYSTEMS and provide food HABITATS for countless ORGANISMS. Their ROOTS help hold water and nutrients in the SOIL. When forests are cut down, RUNOFF waters carry soil and water away, and can eventually result in severe EROSION, or even DESERTIFICATION of the area. [*See also* LOGGING.]

Trophic Level
☙ A part, or level, of a FOOD CHAIN or food web. PRODUC

(continues on p. 112)

Tropical Forests ⚘ FORESTS near

the EQUATOR in areas that have high, constant rainfall and about the same daily temperatures all year. Tropical rainforests are dominated by tall, thin TREES with shallow ROOTS. Their branches form a tight canopy, or leafy covering, that blocks much of the sunlight from reaching the forest floor. Tropical forests include rainforests as well as dry forests, cloud forests, and MANGROVE forests.

Regions. Tropical forests are found near the equator in South America, Central America, Africa, parts of southeast Asia, and some

Tropical forests have a rich diversity of plant and animal species, including many that have not yet been discovered or studied.

Pacific islands. Many forests are found in countries that are facing rapid social and environmental change. The countries are under pressure to provide NATURAL RESOURCES for the rest of the world, with the result that many ENVIRONMENTS have been damaged.

Climate. Tropical areas have a remarkably constant climate. In the tropical rainforest, temperatures may only range from 22°C (72°F) to less than 32°C (90°F) year round. Humidity may be 80 percent or more. Most tropical forests either have frequent rainfall or alternate between dry and wet SEASONS.

Plants. A wealth of plant SPECIES are found in tropical forests. Each region of tropical forest has its own distinct, dominant species. Scientists estimate up to 100 different tree species can be found on only 2.5 acres (1 hectare) of tropical forest land. The forests are dominated by tall trees with shallow roots, smooth trunks, and large, oval leaves.

Plants found under the forest canopy must be able to tolerate shade. One unusual tropical forest plant is the EPIPHYTE, which grows on tree branches and has roots that dangle in the air. Some orchids are epiphytes.

Animals. Tropical forests have a rich diversity of animal species, mostly INSECTS such as ANTS, TER-MITES, and BEETLES. Many animals have unusual sizes, shapes, or colors. There are giant, very colorful butter-flies and beetles as well as many other INVERTEBRATES. Some of the world's most colorful FROGS make tropical forests their homes. PAR-ROTS, hornbills, and toucans are just a few of the many unique tropical for-est BIRDS. MAMMALS are not as di-verse in tropical forests. Among the most common mammals are monkeys and bats. Leopards, tigers, and jaguars are rare CARNIVORES native to tropical forests. Gorillas and chim-panzees are found in the tropical forests of Africa.

Human Impact. Tropical forests are rapidly being destroyed to make way for farms, LOGGING, and other human activities. Deforestation, OVERGRAZING of nearby GRASSLANDS, and the GREENHOUSE EFFECT have also damaged many tropical forests. The result has been a tragic loss of BI-OLOGICAL DIVERSITY. Many experts consider the loss of tropical diversity from HABITAT LOSS to be a critical CONSERVATION issue. [*See also* TREES AND SHRUBS; TROPICS.]

Key Species: Toucan

Toucans are colorful, medium-to-large BIRDS with huge, multicolored bills. They live in the rainforests and forested hills of Mexico, Central America, and northern South America. Noisy birds that live in so-cial groups, toucans nest in holes in trees high in the forest canopy.

Biome Snapshot: Tropical Forests

Geographical Region: Northern South America, Central America, western and central Africa, Madagascar, parts of southeast Asia, Northeast Australia, and on some Pacific islands. **Climate:** Constant warm, humid, moist conditions; average temperatures of about 81°F (27°C); in some areas average tempera-tures reach 84°F (30°C). **Precipitation:** 80 to 95 inches (200 to 240 centimeters), or more, per year; tropical rainforests may have up to 780 inches (2,000 centimeters) of rain per year. **Seasons:** Some areas have distinct wet and dry seasons; others have the same weather all year. **Daylight:** Relatively equal hours of daylight (12 hours) and night (12 hours) every day of the year. **Dominant Plant Life:** Tall trees that form a tight canopy; epiphytes and woody climbing vines such as lianas; each continent has distinct dominant species. **Dominant Animal Life:** Colorful birds; monkeys, jaguars, and tigers; ant, ter-mites, and other insects; amphibians; and bats.

Tropical Grasslands ⚘ GRASS-

LANDS found north and south of TROP-
ICAL rainforests, in areas where PRE-
CIPITATION is too low for many TREES
to grow. They are also called *savannas*. FIRE is an important environmental factor in maintaining tropical
grasslands. It interferes with the
normal process of plant SUCCESSION,
which would eventually lead to
the grasslands being replaced by
FORESTS.

Regions. Tropical grasslands
cover large areas of the interior of
CONTINENTS. The most extensive
tropical grasslands are the savannas
of Africa. The South American grass-

Parts of Africa, including Kenya,
have huge tropical grassland regions
called *savannas* that are filled with
wildlife.

lands, called *llanos*, have a harsher
CLIMATE compared to other tropical
grasslands. The *campos* is a wooded
grassland in Brazil, which has another, flatter savanna called the *pantanal*. Tropical grasslands are also
found in northern Australia and in
parts of India.

Climate. Tropical grasslands are
warm all year. Many areas have very
warm days and much cooler nights.
There are one or two rainy seasons
and one dry period that may reach
drought conditions. Areas with more
rain have more trees and less grass
than other tropical grasslands.

Plants. The dominant plants are
GRASSES, which range from low-
growing forms to SPECIES that reach
10 to 13 feet (3 to 4 meters) high.
Scattered trees are also found. The
type of tree depends on location.
Among the trees found in this biome
are palms, eucalyptus, mesquites,
and acacias.

Animals. There are a large variety of both HERBIVORES and PREDA-
TORS in tropical grasslands. INSECTS
such as ANTS are very common. In
many grasslands, herbivores eat
plants at different heights. ELE-
PHANTS and giraffes, for example, eat
leaves and twigs growing high off the
ground, while the rhinoceros eats
bark and twigs at lower levels. Tropical grasslands often have huge herds

of antelope. Tropical grassland predators include lions, leopards, cheetahs, and wild dogs. There are also many SCAVENGERS such as hyenas, jackals, and vultures.

Human Impact. Many grasslands worldwide have been destroyed by humans to use as farmlands and pastures. Poachers and large game hunters have also slaughtered many grassland animals, such as elephants, the rhinoceros, and large cats. Many tropical grassland animals, as well as the peoples living in grassland areas, are rapidly losing their homes due to habitat destruction. A number of governments have placed large tracts of tropical grasslands under protection as NATIONAL PARKS and WILDLIFE REFUGES. [*See also* TEMPERATE GRASSLANDS; TROPICAL FORESTS; WILDLIFE TRADE.]

Key Species: Cheetah

The cheetah is a large cat that lives in the open plains of the African savanna. Cheetahs have long and slender bodies with small heads and beautiful yellow coats with black spots. Cheetahs stalk prey, mostly gazelles and other HERBIVORES, for a long time before beginning the chase. These graceful cats are able to run at speeds of 75 miles (120 kilometers) per hour over relatively short distances. This is the fastest speed of any land MAMMAL.

Cheetahs are shy animals that do not like changes in their HABITAT. Overhunting and HABITAT LOSS have greatly reduced numbers, and the species is now considered endangered. [*See also* ENDANGERED AND THREATENED SPECIES.]

Biome Snapshot: Tropical Grasslands

Geographical Region: North and south of tropical rainforests, covering large areas of the interior of continents. The most extensive tropical grasslands are in Africa; others are found in South America, Australia and India. **Climate:** Warm all year, with very warm days and cooler nights. **Precipitation:** One or two rainy seasons and one dry period that may reach drought conditions; yearly rainfall ranges from 20 to 59 inches (50 to 150 centimeters). **Dominant Plant Life:** Grasses and, in areas with more rainfall, some trees such as palms, eucalyptus, mesquites, acacias, and the baobab tree. **Dominant Animal Life:** A great variety of herbivores, from ants and other insects to antelope, wildebeests, rhinoceros, hippopotamuses, giraffes, and elephants; many primates, including baboons and mandrills; and large carnivores such as lions, cheetahs, and leopards.

Tundra 🌿 Flat, mostly treeless areas near the Arctic and at the tops of high MOUNTAINS. Tundra covers about 20 percent of the EARTH's land surface. BOGS and MARSHES are common in tundra regions. Tundra SOIL is waterlogged and has a permanently frozen layer called PERMAFROST.

Regions. The arctic tundra is located between the POLAR REGIONS and BOREAL FORESTS of North America, Greenland, Northern Europe, and Northern Asia. Alpine tundra is found at high elevations on some mountains. Alpine tundra in the western United States provides important areas for sheep grazing, mining, and recreational activities such as hiking.

Although the tundra looks quite barren, various plant and animal species are found there.

Climate. The tundra experiences bitter cold temperatures and strong WINDS for most of the year. Winter temperatures can get as low as –94°F (–70°C). The tundra has a short summer lasting only 8 to 10 weeks, when temperatures can get as warm as 85°F (30°C). Little PRECIPITATION falls in arctic tundra, less than 10 inches (25.4 centimeters) per year. More rain and snow falls in alpine tundra, and there are greater daily changes in temperature.

Plants. Windy conditions and a lack of usable water due to the permafrost make the tundra a very difficult place for most plants to live. Only about 360 to 600 plant SPECIES are found in this BIOME. Tundra plants are short and include MOSSES, LICHENS, GRASSES, SEDGES, and dwarf TREES AND SHRUBS.

Animals. Except for summer swarms of flies, mosquitoes, and other flying INSECTS, there are few tundra INVERTEBRATES, AMPHIBIANS, or REPTILES. Three groups of VERTEBRATES live in Arctic tundra: BIRDS, small MAMMALS, and large mammals. Tundra birds include the snowy owl, ptarmigan, geese, and ducks. Small mammals include HERBIVORES, such as lemmings and arctic hares, and CARNIVORES, such as the arctic fox. Large mammals include musk ox, caribou, and polar bears, which are generally found in coastal areas.

More kinds of animals, especially mammals, live in alpine tundra. Among the mammals are chipmunks, ground squirrels, badgers, and red fox. Alpine areas are also home to large mammals such as mule deer, bighorn sheep, mountain goats, and grizzly bears.

Human Impact. Melting ICE, especially in alpine tundra, is a vital source of pure, clean water for humans living at lower ALTITUDES. ERO-SION and mining activities have polluted this natural source of DRINKING WATER, while recreational activities, such as snowmobiling and hiking, have damaged the fragile tundra soil and plant life in some areas.

Key Species: Caribou

The North American caribou and the European and Asian reindeer are different POPULATIONS of the same SPECIES. All three groups live in Arctic tundra. Caribou spend the winter months in the BOREAL FORESTS of Canada but the summer months in the tundra. Herds move hundreds of miles during annual MIGRATIONS. Caribou eat LICHENS and grass.

HABITAT LOSS and excessive hunting caused Alaskan caribou populations to fall from 250,000 in 1970 to only 65,000 in 1976. Since then the population has increased, but future oil development in the Arctic National Wildlife Refuge may destroy more caribou HABITAT and interfere with their annual migrations.

Biome Snapshot: Tundra

Geographical Region: Arctic tundra is located between the polar arctic region and the northern boreal forest biomes. Alpine tundra is found at high elevations of some mountains, at the extreme limits of plant growth. **Climate:** Bitterly cold, with extremely windy conditions; average yearly temperature is −18°F (−8°C); a short summer of 8 to 10 weeks, with longer days and average temperatures around 41°F (5°C). **Precipitation:** Low, less than 10 inches (25.4 centimeters) per year in arctic tundra, mostly as summer rainfall. Alpine tundra has around 4 to 8 inches (10 to 20 centimeters) of snowfall per year. **Seasons:** Long, cold winters and short, cool summers. **Daylight:** No sun in the winter; long days of sunlight in summer, but even then, cloudiness and the fact that the sun is low in the sky causes sunlight to be weak. **Dominant Plant Life:** Lichens, mosses, grasses, sedges, and dwarf trees and shrubs. **Dominant Animal Life:** Snowy owls, lemmings, Arctic fox, musk ox, caribou, grizzly bears, and polar bears in coastal areas.

(continued from p. 105)

ERS, or green PLANTS, form the first trophic level. HERBIVORES, CARNIVORES, and OMNIVORES form higher trophic levels. Except for producers, each trophic level depends on the lower levels for food and energy. Decomposers—organisms that break down and recycle dead materials—and PARASITES—organisms that live on or inside another creature—may obtain food and energy from one or more trophic level. Trophic levels are not precise, and some SPECIES change trophic levels as they grow.

Tropical ✿ Characteristic of, or living in, the TROPICS. The tropics are known for their warm, moist weather, long days, and unchanging climates.

Tropical Forests ✿ *See* PAGE 106.

Tropical Grasslands ✿ *See* PAGE 108.

Tropics ✿ Regions of the EARTH that include areas around the EQUATOR, extending north and south to TEMPERATE zones. The tropics are found between lines of latitude called the Tropic of Cancer to the north and the Tropic of Capricorn to the south. The SUN's rays are felt more intensely in the tropics than in the temperate zones, because the Sun is directly overhead at midday, or close to it. Tropical daylight lasts 11 to 12 hours year-round. The climate does not change much during the year. Average temperatures range from 60 to 80°F (15 to 25°C). Some tropical areas have a dry SEASON followed by a rainy season.

BIOLOGICAL DIVERSITY, or the number of different kinds of ORGANISMS living in an area, is much higher in the tropics than in Earth's other BIOMES. Human activities threaten many tropical SPECIES, however. In addition, many TROPICAL FORESTS and TROPICAL GRASSLANDS have been destroyed for farming and to construct buildings for human use. Tropical OCEANS are home to CORAL REEFS, which are being destroyed by WATER POLLUTION, global warming, fishing boats, and garbage left behind by tourists. [*See also* LATITUDE AND LONGITUDE; LOGGING.]

Troposphere ✿ The lowest layer of the EARTH'S ATMOSPHERE. The troposphere extends from Earth's surface up to an altitude of from 6 to 10 miles (10 to 16 kilometers), where it meets the layer of atmosphere known as the *stratosphere*. Air in the troposphere cools as it approaches the stratosphere. The troposphere holds most of the atmosphere's water vapor and clouds. It is also the site and source of the Earth's strong WINDS and its weather.

Tundra ✿ *See* PAGE 110.

U-Z

Urbanization ⚘ An increase in the number of humans living in cities rather than on farms. Farmers and other rural people tend to have jobs using or harvesting NATURAL RE-SOURCES. City dwellers often have jobs that limit their contact with nature.

Large city POPULATIONS strain a region's resources, and building a city also changes how land is used. WET-LANDS are drained, FORESTS cleared, and natural areas paved. Cities also add to POLLUTION. Because they are separated from nature, city dwellers may forget how important wildlife and nature are to humans.

Veldt ⚘ *See* TEMPERATE GRASSLANDS.

Vertebrates ⚘ ANIMALS with backbones. They include FISH, AMPHIB-IANS, REPTILES, BIRDS, and MAMMALS. Distinctive vertebrate characteristics include hard bone skeletons, the presence of a brain and spinal cord, a head with elaborate sense organs, a complex nervous system, and well-developed heart, liver, and kidneys. Some vertebrates also have highly developed muscular systems. [*See also* APES; BEAVERS; BISON; ELE-PHANTS; FROGS; HUMANS; MARSUPI-ALS; SHARKS AND RAYS; SNAKES; WHALES AND DOLPHINS.]

Volcanoes ⚘ Openings in the EARTH's crust that form when heat and pressure caused mainly by movements of large pieces of crust called *tectonic plates* force lava, gases, ash, and large hot ROCKS to flow or shoot out into the ATMOSPHERE. Some volcanoes slowly ooze, while others undergo explosive eruptions.

Active volcanoes have frequent eruptions. Dormant, or inactive, volcanoes may erupt in the future but have not done so recently. Extinct volcanoes have not erupted for a long time and are not expected to do so in the future. Volcanoes can change local HABITATS dramatically, depositing layers of lava, ash, and rocks. Volcanic eruptions can also affect CLIMATES across the planet. Dust and ash from eruptions can rise into the atmosphere, circle the globe, and block

Active volcanoes, like this one in Costa Rica, deposit layers of lava, ash, and rock.

some of the SUN's rays, causing lower-than-normal temperatures. [*See also* PLATE TECTONICS; SUCCESSION.]

Warm-blooded ⚘ Describes ANIMALS, such as BIRDS and MAMMALS, that are able to keep the same body temperature when air temperatures change. Most scientists use the term *endothermy* to describe an animal that uses an internal mechanism to warm its body. Bird feathers and mammal fur also insulate the body against heat loss during cool weather. To survive really cold nights, some animals such as hummingbirds and bats use *torpor*, a process where they purposely lower body temperatures to conserve energy. Ground squirrels can hibernate, or lower their body temperatures, for several months during the winter. [*See also* COLD-BLOODED.]

Waste Management ⚘ The handling of hazardous or toxic materials dumped by humans into the ENVIRONMENT. HAZARDOUS WASTES are pollutants that can damage ECOSYSTEMS or human health. Some hazardous wastes may catch FIRE, such as gasoline. Others, such as acids, may be corrosive, which means they can eat through different materials. Still other hazardous wastes may explode or cause toxic fumes or smells. Many hazardous wastes, including PESTICIDES and other chemicals, cause serious health problems. Sewage and trash are also types of waste that can harm the environment and human health.

The U.S. federal government has passed a number of laws to help limit the production and release of wastes. These laws are enforced by the Environmental Protection Agency (EPA). For example, the Clean Air Act of 1970 limits the gaseous wastes that companies can emit into the ATMOSPHERE. The Clean Water Act of 1972 limits the kinds and amounts of waste chemicals that companies can release into lakes, rivers, and streams.

Society needs to find other ways to manage waste and its production in

Each year, humans dump tons of waste materials in large landfills like this one.

order to help protect the environment. People can pressure companies to find better ways to handle and dispose of wastes. They can also find environmentally friendly alternatives to toxic household cleaners, fertilizers, and pesticides. [*See also* AIR POLLUTION; POLLUTION; RECYCLING; SUSTAINABLE DEVELOPMENT; WATER POLLUTION.]

Water Cycle ⚘ The process by which water moves among the OCEANS, ATMOSPHERE, and land. It is also called the *hydrological cycle*. Humans depend on the water cycle for pure, clean DRINKING WATER.

The water cycle begins when water in the air falls to earth as rain, sleet, hail, or snow. As heat from the SUN warms the ground and oceans, it causes some of the water to evaporate back into the air. This moisture forms water vapor and clouds. Water from PLANTS returns to the air through the process of TRANSPIRATION. Rain also soaks into the SOIL, where some of it is used by plants and other ORGANISMS. The rest sinks down to form GROUNDWATER. Water that does not evaporate or soak into the ground forms RUNOFF. Water in runoff empties into lakes, streams, and ponds. Groundwater and runoff eventually empty back into the oceans.

The water cycle is vital to all ECOSYSTEMS. Local water conditions are influenced by the water cycle. Water availability determines which plants can live in an area, and a region's plant life often determines which ANIMALS are found there. [*See also* EVAPORATION; NUTRIENT CYCLE.]

Water Pollution ⚘ Contamination that occurs when harmful materials enter lakes, rivers, streams, OCEANS, and GROUNDWATER. Water pollution spoils human DRINKING WATER and can destroy ECOSYSTEMS.

There are several kinds of water pollutants. Untreated human wastes, or sewage, contain germs that can cause serious water pollution. Toxic materials such as mercury, PESTICIDES, and oil released into waterways by industries form another type of water pollution. RUNOFF from construction, mining, and farming sites and from cities are also sources of water pollution.

Healthy water contains ORGANISMS that help keep the water clean by digesting wastes and recycling nutrients. However, if too many pollutants are in the water, this natural cleaning process can no longer keep the water clean. Water pollution can harm PLANTS and FISH, as well as other ANIMALS that drink the water or eat anything that was in it. As a result, it can be very harmful to HABITATS.

Treating industrial waste and sewage can help reduce water pollution. Laws that limit the amount of pollutants that are released in waterways can also help. The U.S. government has passed a number of laws aimed at reducing water pollution in the nation. [*See also* HAZARDOUS WASTE; NATURAL RESOURCES; POLLUTION; RECYCLING; SUSTAINABLE DEVELOPMENT; WASTE MANAGEMENT.]

Watershed ❧ Also called a drainage basin. A watershed is the land that supplies RUNOFF and GROUNDWATER to a system of rivers and streams. Runoff and groundwater from a watershed resupply water lost through EVAPORATION. Nutrients and other materials, as well as SOIL and pollutants, enter and are carried

Acids and other wastes from mining operations often seep into streams, polluting the water.

along with a watershed's waters. A watershed can be small, perhaps only a few acres, or very large, such as the Amazon watershed in South America.

The deep ROOTS and dense PLANT cover found in forested watersheds help to hold nutrients and soil in place. Cutting a FOREST down increases runoff and causes the loss of soil and nutrients through EROSION. URBANIZATION and farming change watersheds in similar ways, increasing the chance of flooding in an area. These changes also cause erosion along streams and rivers and increase WATER POLLUTION. [*See also* WATER CYCLE.]

Water Table ⚑ The top, or upper surface of GROUNDWATER inside the earth. The water table is level, but it follows the shape, or TOPOGRAPHY, of the ground above. When the local topography is low, the water table may be above ground, where it forms streams, lakes, ponds, and WETLANDS. The water table can change over time, sometimes due to human activities. Pumping water out of underground supplies, for example, can cause the water table to fall. [*See also* WATER CYCLE.]

Weather ⚑ *See* CLIMATE AND WEATHER.

Wetlands ⚑ *See* PAGE 118.

Whales and Dolphins ⚑ MARINE MAMMALS with large flippers and no hair. Whales and dolphins are found on the open OCEAN and in coastal waters. They have a large layer of fat, or blubber, that helps keep them warm in cold ocean water. Whales and dolphins often migrate long distances. The blue whale is the largest animal that has ever lived on EARTH.

These MAMMALS belong to one of two groups: toothed whales and baleen whales. Dolphins, porpoises, killer whales, and sperm whales are toothed whales. Killer whales eat FISH, seals, porpoises, and smaller whales. Sperm whales eat giant squid, SHARKS, and other fish. Baleen whales, also called toothless whales, are larger than toothed whales. They have a kind of comb on the inside their mouths that they use to strain tiny INVERTEBRATES out of the water. The right whale and humpback whale are baleen whales.

Whales have been overharvested for their oil and as food. The International Whaling Commission has banned hunting on northern right whales and blue whales, which are ENDANGERED SPECIES. Other vulnerable species include bowhead, fin, humpback, Sei, southern right whales, and gray whales, which need

(continues on p. 120)

Where Are They Found? River Dolphins

River dolphins are unusual because they have long snouts, or noses, and because they live in large rivers in India, Pakistan, South America, and China. River dolphins are small for whales, only 10 feet (1.5 to 2.9 meters) long and weighing just 88 to 276 pounds (40 to 125 kilograms). They have small eyes and poorly developed vision. To find food and avoid barriers, river dolphins probably rely more on echolocation, or bouncing sound waves off objects in the ENVIRONMENT. These interesting animals eat FISH and INVERTEBRATES that live on the muddy river bottoms.

Wetlands ☙

Areas with standing water and often heavy PRECIPITATION. Wetlands form important wildlife HABITATS. They are also important for flood control. Wetland plants can clean water by absorbing pollutants.

Types of Wetlands. There are three types of wetlands: MARSHES, SWAMPS, and BOGS. Marshes have areas of open water and grasslike plants such as SEDGES and reeds.

Swamps are wetlands with TREES AND SHRUBS. In the northeast United States, the typical swamp trees are red maples. The southeast has cypress swamps, with cypress and oak trees. MANGROVE swamps are found in TROPICAL coastal areas.

Bogs are cold wetlands where dead matter does not decompose, or break down, very quickly. The dead material collects and forms peat, which some people use as a fertilizer or burn for fuel. Bogs form when lakes and ponds fill in with SOIL and floating mats of PLANTS. Sphagnum MOSS and short shrubs are common.

Regions and Climate. Wetlands cover about 6 percent of the world's land. They are found around ponds, lakes, and rivers and along COASTLINES. Brazil's Pantanal is the world's largest freshwater wetland. Most wetlands found in the United States are in Alaska.

The climate of wetland varies. Wetlands are distributed worldwide, in areas with standing water and heavy precipitation. Each wetland's climate mirrors that of the local area.

Plants. Wetlands often have water-loving plants that are adapted to grow in waterlogged ground.

Wetlands are important habitats for many species of plants and animals, especially birds. Brigantine Wildlife Refuge in New Jersey teems with different species of birds.

Swamp trees in particular are different from most land plants because they can tolerate being in standing water. Bogs are known for their sphagnum moss. Some human foods, including wild rice, blackberries, and cranberries, grow in wetlands.

Animals. Wetlands are home to many kinds of ANIMALS, including numerous INVERTEBRATES. Mosquitoes and other biting flies are often very abundant, as are frogs, salamanders, box turtles, and water SNAKES. Alligators and crocodiles inhabit wetlands in warmer areas.

Wetlands teem with BIRDS. Wading birds like rails, bitterns, blue herons, and egrets feed on invertebrates. Red-winged blackbirds, swamp sparrows, and marsh wrens nest in wetlands, as do sandhill cranes, ducks and geese.

Wetland MAMMALS include raccoons, muskrats, BEAVERS, and mink. White-tailed deer and moose are also often found in marshes.

Human Impact. Humans use wetland plants, especially berries and rice, as food. They also enjoy wetlands for fishing, hunting, boating, and nature studies. Drainage from irrigated lands and from toxic waste dumps and landfills can lead to a buildup of WATER POLLUTION in wetlands. Wetlands are often drained and converted to homes or farms. The federal government has passed laws to help preserve wetlands from further destruction and misuse. [*See also* FRESHWATER BIOMES; MARINE BIOMES.]

Biome Snapshot: Wetlands

Geographical Region: Cover about 6 percent of the world's land; found around ponds, lakes, and rivers and along seacoasts; many are found in Africa. Brazil's Pantanal is classified as the world's largest freshwater wetland; most wetlands found in the United States are in Alaska. **Climate and Precipitation:** Vary with geographical region; heavy precipitation is a common feature of wetlands. **Seasons and Daylight:** These vary with geographical location. **Dominant Plant Life:** Water-loving plants; swamp trees can tolerate being in standing water; cattails, SEDGES, and reeds in marshes; red maple, cyprus, and mangrove trees in swamps; sphagnum MOSS and pitcher plants in bogs; swamp milkweed, tamarack trees, and white cedar trees in bogs; wild rice, blackberries, cranberries, and blueberries also grow in wetlands. **Dominant Animal Life:** Abundant invertebrates, frogs, salamanders, box turtles, and water snakes; alligators and crocodiles; numerous birds, including wading birds, red-winged blackbirds, cranes, ducks, and geese; raccoons, beavers, muskrats; white-tailed deer and moose.

An intelligent and playful animal, the bottlenose dolphin is the best-known species of dolphin.

(continued from p. 117)

protection from overhunting. Whale populations are also threatened by ships and fishing nets, which sometimes injure them. [*See also* MARINE BIOMES; MIGRATION.]

Wildlife Refuges ♣ PUBLIC LANDS that have been set aside to protect and preserve wildlife. There are three kinds of wildlife refuges: those meant to preserve large ECOSYSTEMS; areas rich in BIOLOGICAL DIVERSITY, such as CORAL REEFS and TROPICAL FORESTS; and reserves set aside to help protect one SPECIES. For example, there are special wildlife refuges for the California condor, African elephants, and giant pandas. Specialized refuges also form havens for other ORGANISMS living within their borders. Although it causes controversy, governments often permit refuges to be used for LOGGING, grazing, hunting, and other recreational activities. [*See also* NATIONAL PARKS; NATURAL RESOURCES; NICHE.]

Wildlife Trade ♣ The sale or purchase of wild animals and other ORGANISMS or their products. Some wild POPULATIONS are threatened by wildlife trade. This destructive practice is driven by people who are willing to pay large sums for rare or exotic animals, furs, medicines made from animal parts, and reptile-skin shoes and handbags. In an attempt to control wildlife trading, the 1990 Convention on International Trade in Endangered Species banned the sale of ocelots, PARROTS, hard coral, and sea turtles. Ivory sales were also banned. [*See also* NATURAL RESOURCES; WILDLIFE REFUGES.]

Wind ♣ Air movement, especially strong air currents. Wind is caused by the movement of cold air into areas where warm air is rising. Large, regular air currents play an important role in global CLIMATE AND WEATHER patterns.

Regional weather systems are also influenced by wind. For example, when large, moist air currents hit

MOUNTAINS, the air is forced upward. As the air rises it also cools, and water vapor may form heavy rains on one side of the mountain. After releasing water vapor, the air is drier. Dry air reaching the other side of the mountain can contribute to DESERT conditions there. Another example of how winds influence local weather occurs when polar wind currents are forced south, where they carry cold, dry air to more TEMPERATE regions.

Although local wind currents vary, they still influence living creatures. Windy conditions increase water loss from living ORGANISMS through EVAPORATION and TRANSPIRATION. Wind is also important for POLLINATION in many PLANTS, especially coniferous TREES. Frequent strong winds can cause plants to become shorter and bushier, and tree

In some areas of the world, wind power has great potential as a renewable energy source. Giant windmills can be used to generate electricity.

branches can be permanently bent to one side by consistent, strong winds. Powerful winds can also knock over trees and other woody plants with shallow ROOTS.

Humans can use wind as a renewable NATURAL RESOURCE. Windmills can be used to pump water and generate electricity without causing POLLUTION.

World Wildlife Fund ⚘ *See* CONSERVATION ORGANIZATIONS.

Worms ⚘ INVERTEBRATES with no arms or legs. There are three broad groups of worms. Flatworms have ribbonlike bodies. They include leeches, a type of PARASITE; and tapeworms, which live inside VERTEBRATES. Roundworms have round bodies with thinner heads and tails. Many are parasites. The third type of worm is the segmented worm, which has a body divided into tiny sections called *segments*. Earthworms are a familiar type of segmented worm. They play an important role in breaking up and aerating SOILS. Worms are found in MARINE BIOMES, FRESHWATER BIOMES, and land biomes.

Zooplankton ⚘ *See* PLANKTON.

Zoos and Aquariums ⚘ Places where people can see and learn about ANIMALS. They play a vital role in edu-

cating people about wildlife and sparking interest in CONSERVATION issues. Zoos generally feature terrestrial, or land-based, animals, including a number of large wild animals from different parts of the world. Aquariums feature a wide range of marine animals, from sponges and corals to sea turtles, SHARKS AND RAYS, and WHALES AND DOLPHINS. Some aquariums specialize in displays of local freshwater PLANTS and animals.

In the past, animals in zoos were often kept in small cages that made it hard to move around, play, or engage in normal behavior. Today, the best zoo exhibits provide large enclosures that look and feel more like the animals' natural HABITATS. Large aquar-

Zoos are important refuges for many threatened species of animals.

iums also include huge tanks that simulate whole marine communities. Such exhibits allow people to see natural animal behaviors.

Zoos and aquariums have also become important refuges for ENDANGERED AND THREATENED SPECIES such as the panda, cheetah, and snow leopard. Some zoos and aquariums have special breeding programs to help captive animals reproduce. However, such efforts are limited by a lack of space, money, and trained caregivers.

Zoos and aquariums also help with research and conservation projects in the wild. In addition, some zoos focus on animal welfare issues, taking in animals that were kept as exotic pets but were abandoned.

Case Study: San Diego Zoo

The 100-acre (40.5 hectare) Zoological Society of San Diego was started in 1916 with just 50 animals from local menageries, or collections. It is now one of the world's finest zoos, housing over 3,800 ANIMALS from 800 SPECIES as well as 6,500 PLANT species. The Center for the Reproduction of Endangered Species (CRES) project at the San Diego Zoo has helped to raise more than 100 cheetahs. Other endangered species helped by CRES include pandas, rhinoceros, and condors.

Selected Bibliography

General

Allaby, Michael. *The Concise Oxford Dictionary of Ecology.* New York: Oxford University Press, 1994.

Black, Matthew, ed. *The Encyclopedia of the Environment.* New York: Franklin Watts, 1999.

Burnie, David. *How Nature Works: 100 Ways Parents and Kids Can Share the Secrets of Nature.* Pleasantville, NY: Reader's Digest, 1991.

Cherry, Lynne. *River Ran Wild: An Environmental History.* New York: Harcourt Brace, 1992.

DK Nature Encyclopedia. New York: DK Publishing, 1998.

Hunken, Jorie. *Ecology for All Ages: Discovering Nature through Activities for Children and Adults.* Old Saybrook, CT: Glove Pequot Press, 1994.

Kellert, Stephen R., ed. *Macmillan Encyclopedia of the Environment.* New York: Macmillan, 1997.

Marshall, Elizabeth L. *High-Tech Harvest: A Look At Genetically Engineered Foods.* New York: Franklin Watts, 1999.

Morgan, Sally, and P. Lalor. *World Food.* New York: Franklin Watts, 1998.

Pringle, Laurence. *The Environmental Movement: From Its Roots to the Challenge of a New Century.* New York: HarperCollins, 2000.

Scott, Michael. *The Young Oxford Book of Ecology.* New York: Oxford University Press, 1998.

Biomes

Arrit, Susan. *The Living Earth Book of Deserts.* Pleasantville, NY: Reader's Digest, 1993.

Baker, Lucy. *Life in Oceans.* New York: Scholastic, 1993.

Bredeson, Carmen. *Tide Pools.* New York: Franklin Watts, 1999.

Clarke, Penny, and Carolyn Scrace. *Beneath the Oceans.* New York: Franklin Watts, 1998.

Delafosse, Claude, and G. Jeunesse. *Caves: Hidden World.* New York: Scholastic, 2000.

Dunphy, Madeleine. *Here Is the African Savanna.* New York: Hyperion Press, 1999.

George, Jean Craighead, and Gary Allen. *One Day in the Tropical Rain Forest.* New York: HarperCollins, 1991.

Gibbons, Gail. *Marshes and Swamps.* New York: Holiday House, 1998.

———. *Nature's Green Umbrella: Tropical Rain Forests.* New York: Morrow, 1997.

Gutnik, Martin J., and Natalie Browne-Gutnik. *Great Barrier Reef.* Austin: Raintree/Steck-Vaughn, 1995.

Hibbert, Adam. *A Freshwater Pond.* New York: Crabtree Publishing, 1999.

Lambert, David. *People of the Grasslands.* Austin: Raintree/Steck-Vaughn, 1998.

———. *The Kingfisher Young People's Book of Oceans.* New York: Larousse Kingfisher Chambers, 1997.

Martin, Patricia A. Fink, et al. *Rivers and Streams.* New York: Franklin Watts, 1999.

Niering, William A. *Wetlands.* New York: Knopf, 1985.

Parker, S., and J. Parker. *Mountains and Valleys.* San Diego: Thunder Bay Press, 1996.

Sayre, April Pulley. *Temperate Deciduous Forest.* Brookfield, CT: Twenty-First Century Books/ Millbrook Press, 1995.

Silver, Donald M., and Patricia J. Wynne. *Arctic Tundra.* New York: McGraw-Hill, 1997.

———. *Coral Reef.* New York: McGraw-Hill, 1997.

———. *Swamp.* New York: McGraw-Hill, 1997.

———. *Woods.* New York: McGraw-Hill, 1997.

Simon, Seymour. *Deserts.* Keighley, Britain: Mulberry Books, 1997.

Climate and Weather

Allaby, Michael. *DK Guide to Weather.* New York: DK Publishing, 2000.

Cosgrove, Brian, et al. *Eyewitness: Weather.* New York: DK Publishing, 2000.

Kahl, Jonathan D. *National Audubon Society First Field Guide: Weather.* New York: Scholastic, 1998.

Taylor, Barbara. *Weather and Climate: Geography Facts and Experiments.* New York: Larousse Kingfisher Chambers, 1993.

Conservation

Brown, Laurie Krasny, and Marc Tolon Brown. *Dinosaurs to the Rescue!: A Guide to Protecting Our Planet.* Boston: Little, Brown, 1994.

Collard, Sneed, et al. *Acting for Nature: What Young People around the World Are Doing to Protect the Environment.* Berkeley, CA: Heyday Books, 2000.

Gibbons, Gail. *Recycle: A Handbook for Kids.* Boston: Little, Brown, 1996.

Morgan, Sally. *Acid Rain.* New York: Franklin Watts, 1999.

National Wildlife Federation. *Pollution: Problems and Solutions.* New York: McGraw-Hill, 1998.

The Earth

Bang, Molly Garrett. *Common Ground: The Water, Earth and Air We Share.* New York: Scholastic, 1997.

Redfern, Martin. *The Kingfisher Young People's Book of Planet Earth.* New York: Larousse Kingfisher Chambers, 1999.

Ricciuti, Edward R. and Margaret W. Carruthers. *National Audubon Society First Field Guide: Rocks and Minerals.* New York: Scholastic, 1998.

Simon, Seymour. *Icebergs and Glaciers.* New York: Mulberry Books/HarperCollins, 1999.

The Visual Dictionary of the Earth. New York: DK Publishing, 1993.

Life and Its Changes

Burnie, David. *Eyewitness: Life.* New York: DK Publishing, 1999.

Kalman, Bobbie, and Jacqueline Langille. *What Are Food Chains and Webs?* New York: Crabtree Publishing/Perfection Learning Corp., 1998.

———. *What Is a Life Cycle?* New York: Crabtree Publishing/Perfection Learning Corp., 1998.

Plants and Animals

Behler, John L. *National Audubon Society First Field Guide: Reptiles.* New York: Scholastic, 1999.

Burnie, David. *The Kingfisher Illustrated Encyclopedia of Animals.* New York: Larousse Kingfisher Chambers, 1992.

Cassie, Brian, and Majorie Burns. *National Audubon Society First Field Guide: Trees.* New York: Scholastic, 1999.

Cassie, Brian. *National Audubon Society First Field Guide: Amphibians.* New York: Scholastic, 1999.

Chinery, Michael. *Plants and Planteaters.* New York: Crabtree Publishing, 2000.

Grassy, John, et al. *National Audubon Society First Field Guide: Mammals.* New York: Scholastic, 1998.

Kalman, Bobbie. *What Is a Plant?* New York: Crabtree Publishing, 2000.

Lessem, Don. *Dinosaurs to Dodos: An Encyclopedia of Extinct Animals.* New York: Scholastic, 1999.

O'Toole, Christoper. *Encyclopedia of Insects.* New York: Checkmark Books, 1995.

Savage, Steven. *Animals of the Rain Forest.* Austin: Raintree/Steck-Vaughn, 1999.

Smith, C. Lavett. *National Audubon Society First Field Guide: Fishes.* New York: Scholastic, 2000.

Suzuki, David, and Barbara Hehner. *Looking at Plants.* New York: John Wiley & Sons, 1992.

Weidensaul, Scott. *National Audubon Society First Field Guide: Birds.* New York: Scholastic, 1998.

Whitfield, Phillip. *The Simon & Schuster Encyclopedia of Animals: A Visual Who's Who of the World's Creatures.* New York: Simon & Schuster, 1998.

Wilsdon, Christina. *National Audubon Society First Field Guides: Insects.* New York: Scholastic, 1998.

Major Organizations and Agencies

Earthwatch
680 Mount Auburn Street
P.O. Box 9104
Watertown, MA 02471-9104
(617) 925-8200
www.earthwatch.org

Environmental Defense Fund
257 Park Avenue South, 16th Floor
New York, NY 10010
(212) 505-2100
www.edf.org

Environmental Protection Agency
401 M Street SW
Washington, DC 20460
(202) 260-2090
www.epa.gov

Fish and Wildlife Service
Department of the Interior
Main Interior Building
Washington, DC 20240
(202) 208-4131
www.fws.gov

Friends of the Earth
1026 Vermont Avenue NW, Suite 300
Washington, DC 20005
(202) 783-7400
www.foe.org

Greenpeace USA
1436 U Street NW
Washington, DC 20009
(202) 462-1177
www.greenpeaceusa.org

Kids for a Clean Environment
P.O. Box 158254
Nashville, TN 37215
(615) 331-7381
www.kidsface.org

National Audubon Society
700 Broadway
New York, NY 10003
(212) 979-3000
www.audubon.org

National Geographic Society
1145 17th Street NW
Washington, DC 20036
(202) 857-7000
www.nationalgeographic.com

National Parks and Conservation Association
1776 Massachusetts Avenue NW
Washington, DC 20036
(800) 628-7275
ww.npca.org

National Park Service
Department of the Interior
Main Interior Building
1849 C Street NW
Washington, DC 20240
(202) 208-3100
www.nps.gov

National Wildlife Federation
8925 Leesburg Pike
Vienna, VA 22184
(800) 822-9919
www.nwf.org

Rainforest Alliance
65 Bleecker Street
New York, NY 10012-2420
(212) 677-1900
www.rainforest-alliance.org

Sierra Club
85 Second Street
San Francisco, CA 94105
(415) 977-5500
www.sierraclub.org

Wilderness Society
900 17th Street NW
Washington, DC 20006
(800) 843-9453
www.wilderness.org

Wildlife Conservation Society
2300 Southern Boulevard
Bronx, NY 10460
(718) 220-6891
www.wcs.org

World Wildlife Fund
1250 24th Street NW, Suite 400
Washington, DC 20037
(202) 293-4800
www.worldwildlife.org

Index

Page numbers for main entries (including feature box titles) are in bold face. Page numbers for illustrations are in italics.